Sea Trout Run

Sea Trout Run

Peter Jarrams

A&C Black · London

Angling may be said to be so like mathematics that it can never be fully learnt.

Izaak Walton
'The Compleat Angler'

First published 1987 by
A & C Black (Publishers) Limited
35 Bedford Row, London WC1R 4JH

Jarrams, Peter
  Sea trout run.
  1. Trout
  I. Title
  597'.55   QL638.S2
  ISBN 0-7136-5584-4

Printed and bound in Great Britain by
A. Wheaton & Co. Ltd, Exeter

Contents

Acknowledgements

I am most grateful for the assistance I have received in the preparation of this work and I would like to thank the following in particular.

Malcolm Davies assisted in collecting scale samples and approached much of the photographic work with considerable enthusiasm. I am indebted to him for photographs on pages 14, 69, 74, 75, 87, 95, 107 and 119. I would also like to thank Jim Waltham for providing the cover photograph (showing Lock Iel). The photomicrographs of sea trout scales on page 16 were produced by Geoff Wheatley. The photographs on pages 44 and 45 are the work of Adrian Stephens. Ian Peters' assistance in photograph selection was invaluable. Several of the tables are compiled from information contained in the *Annual Fisheries Reports* of the Regional Water Authorities—the Welsh Water Authority: tables 4 and 7; the Northumbrian Water Authority: table 3; the South West Water Authority: table 6; and the Yorkshire Water Authority: table 2. The Electricity Supply Board of Ireland (E.S.B.) allowed me to reproduce table 9 from their 1979 fisheries report.

To all my friends on the river bank whose ever cheerful greetings make the sport that much more enjoyable.

Introduction

Many books have been written about the king of fish, the Atlantic salmon. However, a large proportion of them contain only a throw-away chapter or two, usually the last, on sea trout, almost as a dismissal of this close cousin. The sea trout is worthy of a more detailed scrutiny of its life style and the angling methods which need to be employed for its capture, so different in many ways from those used for salmon. In *Life of the Sea Trout* G. H. Nall redresses the balance a little and gives an account of British populations, which is based almost entirely on the results of scale readings. Hugh Falkus also provides further angling information in *Sea Trout Fishing*. Apart from these two publications it is a struggle to recall an authoritative work, except for a few detailed scientific investigations.

If the salmon is king, then surely the sea trout is a prince among fish? In many areas the decline in the salmon runs, for various reasons, has become a serious threat to future stocks. The sea trout, with some annual fluctuations, seem to be able to maintain population numbers and are becoming increasingly important in districts where the salmon runs are diminishing. Perhaps the prince will one day become the king!

This book is written by an angler for anglers. As well as sections on fishing methods and how to apply them, there is also detailed information on the biology and habitat requirements for sea trout. As in any form of hunting, an understanding of the quarry—its habits, likes and dislikes —is important if the hunter is to be at all successful.

The forms of angling described are many and varied, and little or no distinction is made between the moral or sporting values of the techniques employed, though attempts are made to explain some prejudices. Angling is a recreational activity, carried out, in the main, for an individual's personal enjoyment. Bearing in mind the availability or proximity of the different types of angling, each branch has its own particular attraction and devotees. For instance, to catch salmon or sea trout on a fly is considered, in some circles, to be the ultimate in angling experiences. The person who does so, however, may not necessarily enjoy his or her sport any more than the angler who fishes with a worm in a flood for the same fish. Reservoir trout angling, coarse fishing and all the other branches of this varied sport, therefore, have their place and appeal to those people who choose to pursue them.

To become a successful angler, that is, one who is consistently successful, requires a considerable amount of experience, not only of methods and
tackle but also of the fish's lifestyle. Getting to know likely looking lies, the
best times of day, weather and water conditions and the fish's behavioural
patterns are all important. Beginner's luck probably applies to angling
more than to any other sport, but to be consistently 'lucky' requires a level
of skill that only a small proportion of anglers will ever achieve. It is true
that 10 per cent of the anglers catch 90 per cent of the fish, but that is not
to say that the person who catches several hundred sea trout in a season
derives more pleasure than the one who catches half a dozen.

The truly skilful angler is surely the one who, on reaching the water,
surveys the scene, mulls over the prospects and decides to fish by a method
which he considers will catch fish under the prevailing conditions. Those
who stick to just one form of angling may miss out on a large number of
occasions.

My angling time is spent in trying to catch fish by any method, fair and
legal, I consider appropriate to the situation. I enjoy good weather, the
scenery, the wild animals and birds, and the wholesome chat of fellow
anglers, but most of all I enjoy the fishing. I am only there for one real
purpose, and that is to be successful in my efforts—efforts in tempting a
quarry I know to be wary, clever and far more intelligent than many people
realise. The successful angler carrying a nice fish back to his car is at peace
with the world, all his troubles are forgotten and there is a spring in his
step so easy to recognise. If this work should in any small way assist its
reader in experiencing such angling euphoria, then it will have served its
purpose.

Lastly, apart from fishing on the west coast of America for 'steelhead',
the west of Ireland for 'white trout', the south of England for 'peal' and the
Lake District for 'herling', almost all of my angling experience is confined
to south and west Wales. Here the sea trout, or 'sewin' as they are known
locally, are abundant and in most rivers are a more important species than
the salmon, both to anglers and to commercial fishermen. This book,
therefore, centres on the sea trout of Wales where, once a taste of 'sewin
fever' has been sampled, the appeal of these most sporting of fish cannot
be subdued.

Author's note

Many rivers in Wales have names in both English and Welsh. To avoid
confusion to the reader each river mentioned has been given its most easily
identifiable name. For example, the English spelling of Ayron and Teify
has largely died out and so the Welsh Aeron and Teifi are preferred in the
text. Conversely, the Welsh spelling of rivers such as Dyfi and Tywi may
be confusing to the reader from across the border, whereas the more usual
Dovey and Towy make the location of these streams more readily understood.

1
The Sea Trout and its Environment

The Salmon Family

The sea trout, *Salmo trutta*, belongs to the salmonid family which in the British Isles consists of salmon, sea trout, brown trout, American brook trout and char.

Rainbow trout and American brook trout are not natives, although they are now widespread in this country, particularly in lakes and reservoirs. They both originate from North America, brook trout from the Atlantic east coast and rainbow from the Pacific west coast. There are no known sea-migrating populations of either of these species in the British Isles even though there are sea run forms where they occur naturally.

Char, sometimes referred to as Arctic char, inhabit deep, cold water lakes and their distribution is limited to a few mountain lakes in some parts of Wales, the Lake District and Scotland. Again, there are no races that migrate to the sea, as they do in some northern European countries.

The salmon, of which there is only one species native to Britain, the Atlantic salmon, *Salmo salar*, is entirely anadromous. This means it spawns in fresh water, the young fish spend some time in the river feeding and growing until they move out to the sea, and then they return to fresh water once more to spawn as adults. Oddly enough, there are populations of Atlantic salmon which do not migrate to the sea. They spend the whole of their lives in fresh water in several countries, most notably in Scandinavia and eastern North America, but such a phenomenon does not occur in the British Isles.

Perhaps the strangest feature of this diverse and highly adaptable family of fish is that two apparently very different fish are, in fact, the same species and have no difference whatsoever in their physical form. *Salmo trutta*, the brown trout, is also *Salmo trutta*, the sea trout. One form, the brown trout, spends its entire life in fresh water and does not grow very large, except in a few of the bigger rivers and lakes where a two- or three-pound fish is considered a good catch. The other form of this remarkable fish, the sea trout, is migratory and follows a similar lifestyle to that of the salmon. It grows much larger, often to a weight of ten pounds or more, and these large fish will enter quite small rivers to spawn. It is often suggested that the change in habit still takes place between the two types and that the offspring of some brown trout become sea trout, and

9

vice versa. It is known that young sea trout prevented from leaving fresh water revert to brown trout, but normally each breeds true and the offspring adopt the lifestyle of the parents. It is possible that in the wild, crosses between the two do occur (in the hatchery it is easily done for the chromosome count is the same). The young fish are then presumably left to choose either to remain in the river and suffer the rigours of drought, flood and food shortages or to go to sea and sample the freedom and abundant food stores, but where sudden death is just as easily encountered.

Identification

Sea trout are very similar in appearance to salmon, though to the experienced observer they are a quite different fish. However, the difference between them when they are freshly-run fish (recently entered from the sea) can be difficult to distinguish. Each year there is no doubt that many large sea trout which are caught are mistakenly identified as salmon. It is less common for small salmon to be thought of as sea trout, since it would seem that some anglers feel it is far more prestigious to catch the former than the latter. On several occasions I have met a successful angler on the river bank with a fish weighing five or six pounds, and no amount of detailed explanation has persuaded him that his fish was not a salmon but a sea trout. I particularly remember one visiting angler on the Teifi, with a lovely fish of just over four pounds. Nothing would convince him that that fish was a sea trout (which it most certainly was) and he soon left, most annoyed and seeming to take offence as though I had doubted his ability as an angler. A few weeks later I met him again on the river bank and his face beamed with satisfaction as he told me that he had taken some scales off the fish and sent them to his local university where they had pronounced the fish a salmon. He was content with his catch and I suppose that is what angling is all about, but it does show how even experts can make mistakes.

There are several differing features between the two fish. Adult sea trout have a thicker caudal peduncle or tail wrist than a salmon. If, when grasped and held up by the tail, a large fish slips through the hand it is almost certainly a sea trout: although it is relatively simple to tail a salmon after some practice, it is virtually impossible to hand tail a heavy sea trout.

The scale count from the rear of the adipose fin to the lateral line at an angle down and forwards is between thirteen and sixteen (most commonly fourteen) in the sea trout. The same count for salmon is between ten and thirteen, almost invariably eleven. From this it can be seen that the sea trout has more, and smaller, scales. Commercial coracle fishermen on the Taf and Towy in South Wales are able to tell the difference in the dark (the normal time for coracle fishing) by running the inside of the fingers along the fish's flank. The smaller scales of the sea trout have a smoother feel than the salmon's larger and correspondingly rougher textured scales.

Sea trout are, in general, endowed with a much greater number of spots. On adult fish these are scattered all over the upper parts of the body,

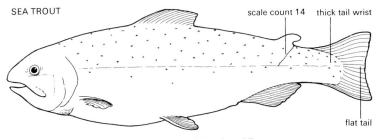

SEA TROUT

scale count 14   thick tail wrist

flat tail

many spots, some below lateral line

SALMON

scale count 11   slim tail wrist

forked tail

few spots, rarely below lateral line

Differences between mature sea trout and salmon

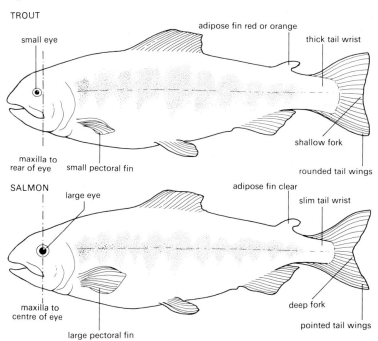

TROUT

small eye

adipose fin red or orange   thick tail wrist

maxilla to
rear of eye   small pectoral fin

shallow fork

rounded tail wings

SALMON

large eye

adipose fin clear   slim tail wrist

maxilla to
centre of eye

large pectoral fin

deep fork

pointed tail wings

Differences between juvenile trout and salmon

A brown trout (top), a sea trout smolt (middle) and a salmon smolt (bottom)

though not normally on the fins, tail or the top of the head. (Spots on the fins and the head are an identifying feature of rainbow trout.) Often these spots will extend to well below the lateral line. Adult salmon have considerably fewer spots and they rarely extend below the lateral line.

It is impossible to tell the difference between young sea trout parr and small brown trout, as they are the same fish. The sea trout, once it is large enough (usually about six inches or fifteen centimetres), will lose its parr marks which are distinctive oval dark marks on the flanks, will turn a silvery colour and will migrate down to the sea. The brown trout will gradually lose its parr marks as it gets older, but will remain coloured and spotted and will continue its life cycle in the river.

Juvenile salmon, which also have these parr marks, are very similar to young trout and are easily confused. The most readily identifiable feature is the colour of the adipose fin—the small boneless fin just forward of the tail, which is peculiar to the salmonid family and is a unique feature of it. The adipose fin of the trout is always coloured a shade of red or orange, even after the fish has grown into a smolt, but the salmon's adipose fin is clear and colourless, usually a light shade of grey.

The maxilla or jaw bone, the long bony plate at each side of the upper jaw, extends beyond a vertical line from behind the eye in the sea trout. The young salmon's mouth is smaller and the maxilla only extends to the mid point of the eye or slightly further. This difference is lost in later life and is not a reliable source of identification in adult fish.

A young trout's tail is only lightly forked and the wing ends are rounded. The salmon parr's tail, however, is deeply forked and the wing ends are pointed. Small salmon grilse (one sea winter fish) often have a tail which is still markedly forked but sea trout of the same size will have an almost flat-edged tail.

The pectoral fins of salmon parr are larger than the trout's and will sometimes extend back to a line drawn vertically with the leading edge of the dorsal fin. This differing feature is also lost in later life. Lastly, the general appearance of salmon parr and smolts is much sleeker than the sturdy profile of the trout.

Scales

Probably the best means of identification of adult fish is an examination of the scales. The scales do not actually differ in any composite way, but the information obtained by 'reading' them provides the history of the fish's lifestyle which, in turn, enables the examiner to identify either a salmon or a sea trout. It is surprising just how much information about a particular fish's life history can be acquired by studying these thin bony plates. All the scales form on the body at the fry stage and grow progressively larger as the fish increases in size. As the fish grows, concentric rings, known as circuli, are laid down around the edge of each scale. When the fish is growing fast, usually in the summer or whilst at sea, the space between the rings is relatively larger than in winter when the fish is growing more slowly. Corresponding summer and winter bands are formed and can be readily identified as such. By counting the number of these seasonal bands in both the fresh water portion of the scale (the centre) and the outer section of salt water growth, the fish's age can be determined.

On the scales of salmon or sea trout the slow river growth at the juvenile stage shows as a massed collection of rings at the centre and the larger sea growth rings are easily identifiable thereafter.

Fresh-run fish from the Teifi: a 4½ lb sewin (top) and a 6 lb grilse (bottom)

*A late season 4 lb sewin from the Towy at Llandovery. A scale
from this fish is illustrated in the photograph on page 16.*

Both species, on reaching maturity and entering fresh water, cease to
feed. This period may extend from several weeks around spawning time
for brown trout to several months for salmon, which do not feed in fresh
water, or for sea trout which may feed in fresh water but, at the adult stage,
generally do not. At this stage of fasting the fish must call on their bodily
reserves and draw calcium from the scales, which results in erosion of the
outermost rings. Once growth again takes place, such as after return to the
sea as a kelt, new rings are laid down around the scarred tissues, leaving
a distinctive mark corresponding to its period of fasting. This is known as
a spawning mark, although it is no indicator that the fish has actually
spawned, only that it has spent some time back in fresh water and has most
probably done so.

When obtaining a sample of scales for examination they should be taken
from the shoulder of the fish in front of the dorsal fin and above the lateral
line. These are the first scales to be laid down when the fish is small and
are, therefore, the largest. They are also in a position where they are least
likely to be damaged. If a scale is lost another grows in its place very
quickly to cover the unprotected area. Such a scale cannot repeat the life
history and is, therefore, blank. For this reason at least half a dozen scales
should be taken to ensure that there is a good readable sample among
them.

The scales should be placed in an envelope and marked with the date,
where the fish was caught, and its length, weight and sex. When required
to be read they are soaked in water and any dirt or mucus removed by
lightly rubbing the surface between the fingers. They are then carefully
placed between two clean glass slides and looked at under a microscope or
a special type of projector which throws an image on to the wall or a screen.

The clearest scale in the sample should be chosen, making sure that it is complete and not regenerated with the resulting blank centre. With experience the art of scale reading can be developed to provide much interesting information, even to the extent of back-calculating a fish's size to a particular stage of its life.

Materials can easily be set up at home, and as well as using the method as a means of fish identification, it can give many hours of pleasure in studying one's own catches and thereby learning more about their life history. It will be quickly learned that a sea trout of six pounds will show two or more spawning marks, whereas a salmon of similar size will probably be a maiden grilse and a much younger fish.

A beautifully marked 7 lb male sewin from the Teifi

An Aeron grilse of 5 lb. Note the slim tail wrist and the deeply forked tail.

Sea trout scales. Top left: *2.0 +* *whitling, weight 13 oz (from bottom fish illustrated on page 95).* Top centre: *2.0 + SM +* *previous spawner, weight 2 lb 6 oz (from top fish illustrated on page 95).* Top right: *2.1 +* *sea trout, weight 1 lb 8 oz (from middle fish illustrated on page 95).* Left: *2.2 +* *sea trout maiden, weight 4 lb (from fish illustrated on page 14).*

Anatomy

Fish are extremely well adapted to living in an underwater environment and differ considerably from land animals in their shape, structure and bodily functions. The sea trout, as all salmonids, is an active, muscular, streamlined fish with keen eyesight to enable it to locate and capture its prey. The features of its anatomy which are particularly important to its lifestyle are:

The muscles The muscles (the flesh that is eaten) make up more than 60 per cent of the body weight. By alternately shortening and flexing the muscles of each flank, which in turn moves the tail from side to side and pushes water backwards, the fish is propelled forwards. A man wearing flippers propels himself in a similar way, but by no means as efficiently. The fins, especially the pectorals (the first paired fins behind the head), are moved by their own independent muscles and enable directional movements to be made, providing both stability and balance.

Sea trout are among the strongest of swimmers and can jump weirs and obstructions or swim through fast currents and mountain torrents to reach their spawning ground. Steady and prolonged swimming speeds (three to four miles per hour) can be maintained for long periods. Short bursts of speed can be made up to five yards per second (about ten m.p.h.), though this depends on the size of the fish and the temperature of the water. In practical terms this means that fish of about two pounds or more in weight

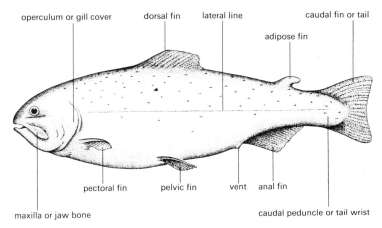

External features of a sea trout

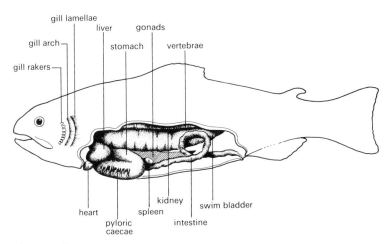

Anatomy of a sea trout

are able to swim up a vertical waterfall three feet (one metre) high, provided that there is enough volume of water to swim through. Falls which are too high to swim up are 'jumped' by using the hydraulic wave —the upwelling boil at the foot of the fall which the fish uses to assist its upward swimming motion at burst speed, thereby allowing it to jump clear of the water. A combination of both swimming and jumping may be used to surmount difficult obstacles.

In its early parr life in the river and later in the sea the burst speed is frequently used to escape from predators or alternatively to catch prey.

Respiration and circulation To sustain life, oxygen must be obtained from the surrounding water and it is essential, therefore, that the water be well oxygenated. Oxygen will dissolve in water naturally from the air, and when water has taken up as much oxygen as it will hold it is said to be saturated. This saturation level varies because the warmer the water becomes, the less oxygen it will hold. For example, at 10°C (50°F) water will be saturated at eleven parts per million (expressed scientifically as eleven milligrams per litre or 11 mg/l). Sea trout would become decidedly uncomfortable if the level dropped to 6 p.p.m. and would die at 4.5 p.p.m. or lower.

Oxygen is obtained by way of the gills. The thin layer of cells covering the gill filaments, or lamellae, allows the dissolved oxygen in the water to pass into the small blood capillaries they contain and the waste carbon dioxide to be dispersed. There are thousands of these lamellae, which provide a vast surface area (more than 50 per cent of the surface area of the fish itself) for the required amount of oxygen to be taken up. It is important not to damage these delicate structures on the gills, for the walls are so thin that the slightest abrasion will cause a rupture and consequent heavy bleeding. I have often seen anglers actually ripping out complete gill sections when unhooking a fish that is intended to be returned. A fish so treated will almost certainly die, since it cannot stand any amount of damage to these delicate and vital organs. It should always be remembered that today's parr is tomorrow's sea trout.

By opening its mouth the fish draws in water. Then, by closing the gullet and closing the mouth in a gulping fashion, the water is forced through the operculum or gill covers at each side and over the gills. This process continues in a similar fashion to that of a terrestrial air-breathing animal, though instead of breathing in and out through the mouth a fish, in effect, breathes in all the time. Gill rakers, bony projections forward of the gill arches (the lamellae supports), ensure that the gills are kept free of food particles when the fish is feeding and guide its food down the gullet.

When a fish is taken out of the water all the lamellae close together in a mass and so there is not enough surface area to absorb the required amount of oxygen. The fish then dies from shortage of 'breath'. As a human being drowns under water, being unable to breathe naturally, a fish drowns out of water for the same reason. The oxygenated blood from the gills passes to all parts of the body through a system of arteries and capillaries and returns to the heart via the veins where the deoxygenated blood is pumped back to the gills. This is a single circulatory system, whereas in mammals it is a double system, the blood travelling from the lungs to the heart, from there to all parts of the body, and then back to the heart before being pumped once more to the lungs.

The swim bladder The swim bladder is characteristic of the bony fishes, or 'teleosts' as they are known scientifically. It is a gas-filled sac contained inside the body cavity beneath the backbone and is responsible for regulating the fish's buoyancy, which will vary with the depth at which it is swimming. It can be deflated or inflated as required by special glands or by actually squeezing out air through the throat, and enables the fish to maintain station with little effort at any depth of water.

Sea fishermen will have seen the swim bladder protrude from the mouth of fish that have been reeled up from deep water. This is because the fish does not have sufficient time to deflate the bladder as it is brought up to an area of much lower pressure, and so the sac expands accordingly.

The kidney The kidney is a long, dark red organ which runs along the length of the underside of the back bone and above the swim bladder. It has the same function as the kidney in mammals and is used to regulate disposal of waste products. It has a much more complicated role in fish, however, for it also serves to counteract the osmotic effect that fish are subject to through being continually immersed in a liquid. When in fresh

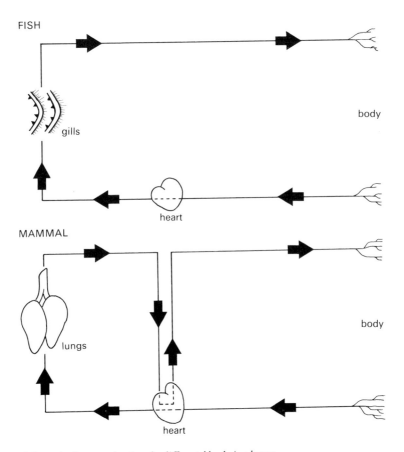

Schematic diagram showing the different blood circulatory systems in fish and in mammals

water, the fish's body, due to osmosis, is always being invaded by absorbed water. The continual intake of water must be counterbalanced by disposal through the urinary tube via the kidneys. In salt water (sea water being stronger than the fish's body salts) the opposite effect takes place. The fish loses body fluid into the surrounding water and it must conserve fluids to prevent it becoming dehydrated. Its kidneys, therefore, now work in reverse.

It is obvious that a fish like the sea trout has to undergo major functional body changes when transferring from fresh water to salt water and the other way round. Only a few other fish are able to cope with this change —salmon, flounders, mullet and eels being the most notable, all of which can and do live in both fresh and salt water. The change may be fairly easy and gradual in larger rivers with long estuarine reaches where the salt water and fresh water mix gradually. Whether travelling to or from the river, the fish can remain for a period in brackish water, if it so desires, to acclimatize itself to the changing water. Rivers which empty directly into the sea must, however, create a major problem by providing such a sudden and dramatic change. This may explain the wild and drunken nature of some fish after freshly entering a river.

The lateral line A sea trout's ears are inside the skull and are poorly developed, but it is able to pick up sound vibrations in the water through the lateral line. This important sensory organ is seen as a dark line running the length of the body more or less at a mid point from just behind the gills to the tail. If examined closely, small holes can be seen in the scales along its length. These holes allow vibrations in the water to pass through to the sensitive nerve cells underneath. Not only sounds are detected; other fish or predators' movements nearby can be sensed and it is also quite possible that the fish can detect distances from moving and stationary objects in a similar fashion to an echo sounder or radar. It must be invaluable to a fish in dirty water, such as when it is finding its way upstream in a flood.

The digestive system Like other predatory fish (the carnivores) the sea trout swallows its food whole and usually still alive. It has no pharyngeal teeth in the throat for mastication, as do coarse fish like carp which chew their food. The stomach is large to accommodate prey food and once the prey is killed by the acid present it is quickly broken down into smaller digestible particles. Since animal food is easily digested the intestine is short, as opposed to that of herbivorous (plant-eating) fish which is considerably longer to cope with the difficult digestion of vegetable matter. To the rear of the stomach lie the pyloric caecae which are an important aid to digestion processes. They are pale, long, thin tubes which look very much like a small bunch of worms. They are often mistaken for gut parasites and may be one of the reasons why modern housewives find the gutting of fish a distasteful task.

The liver and the pancreas also play an active part in the process of digestion by producing juices which further break down the food particles and ultimately convert them into energy or growth.

The reproductive system The anatomy of the reproductive system is briefly described here but the actual reproduction process is described in detail in the chapter about the sea trout's life cycle. When the fish is immature or between spawnings, the ovaries of the female or the testes of the male (I have never liked calling fish cocks or hens as though pheasants or farmyard fowls) are small and difficult to see among the other belly contents. As they mature these organs enlarge considerably and in a female sea trout just before spawning the ovaries may amount to as much as 20 per cent of its body weight.

The female ovaries consist of two sacs full of eggs or ova. These sacs are orange or yellow in colour and lengthen and expand as spawning time approaches to fill the whole of the available space in the body cavity. In the male, the gonads or testes similarly grow, though not quite so large, and they are seen as a pair of swollen, creamy white, longitudinal sacs.

Water Quality and Habitat Requirements

Dissolved oxygen Nearly all plants and animals need to 'breathe' oxygen under water and it is essential to fish life. As already explained, the warmer the water the less oxygen it is able to hold, but there are factors other than temperature which can govern the amount of oxygen dissolved in it. Submerged plant life, through a process known as photosynthesis, gives off oxygen into the surrounding water during the day. During respiration at night, oxygen is used up by plants and carbon dioxide is given off, with the result that heavily weeded waters can become seriously depleted of oxygen, particularly just before dawn. This condition rarely occurs in sea trout rivers but can be a problem if the rivers become very

Table 1: 100% saturation values for dissolved oxygen in fresh water at different temperatures.

Temp °C	Mg/l	Temp °C	Mg/l
0	14.63	13	10.53
1	14.23	14	10.29
2	13.84	15	10.07
3	13.46	16	9.86
4	13.11	17	9.65
5	12.77	18	9.46
6	12.45	19	9.27
7	12.13	20	9.08
8	11.84	21	8.91
9	11.55	22	8.74
10	11.28	23	8.57
11	11.02	24	8.42
12	10.77	25	8.26

low and choked with weed, as happened in the drought summers of 1947 and 1976. In the slower moving reaches of the river where little oxygenation takes place it can drop to as low as 45 per cent of saturation, the point at which some fish deaths will occur. Another reason for oxygen depletion is pollution. Quite often a cause of fish deaths can be traced to some form of organic pollution, such as farm effluent from cow sheds, creamery waste or sewage. The waste itself is not poisonous or injurious to the fish but fish will die because of a lack of dissolved oxygen. It has all been used up by the multitude of small organisms feeding on the polluting matter. Water quality scientists can measure the amount of pollution in a water by calculating the 'biochemical oxygen demand' (BOD) and in Britain BOD standards are set for factory discharges, effluents, sewage outfalls, etc., to guard against the possible effects of polluting waters and the resulting oxygen depletion.

Temperature Different species of fish can only live within certain limits of temperature. For sea trout these limits are from 0°C to about 22°C (32° to 72°F). They are cold-blooded animals and their body temperature is the same as, and changes with, the surrounding water temperature. They cannot, however, stand sudden changes in temperature of more than a few degrees and death will occur at around 22°C, unless the change has been very gradual when they may become acclimatized to higher temperatures but will not be able to tolerate such for any length of time. As the fish's metabolic rate (bodily functions of breathing, circulation and digestion) increases with temperature, so its body requires more oxygen. As the warmer water holds less oxygen, this can be a major cause of death at the higher lethal limits of temperature. Optimum efficiency of growth and health lies between about 10°C and 14°C, though a lower temperature of around 6°C to 8°C is required for spawning.

pH pH is a measure of the alkalinity or acidity of water. The scale runs from 1 to 14, with low numbers being acidic, high numbers alkaline, and pH7 neutral. The pH of rivers is generally governed by the terrain through which they flow. Chalk streams and rivers that flow through limestone areas, as are found in southern England, have a high pH, are most productive waters for animal and plant life, and have many and varied species. Growth of fish is fast, owing to the abundant food supply; hence the excellent brown trout fishing in chalk streams like the Test and Itchen.

Acid streams, sometimes associated with peat bogs, or hard non-porous rocks with thin soils, are found in parts of Scotland and Ireland. They are unproductive waters, containing few species of plant and animal life, and the growth of fish in such waters is slow. In north-west and south-west England and in Wales rivers are normally of a neutral or near neutral pH. This is sea trout country and they do best in such neutral type waters.

Different species of fish have different tolerance levels to pH. Salmonids prefer the range 6.5 to 8 but can survive to limits of 4.5 and 9. Outside these figures some deaths will occur but, like temperature change, if it is gradual it is possible for fish to become acclimatized. Fish are, however, less able to withstand a sudden change in pH than in temperature and a rapid change of two points or more usually results in death. Some of the coarse fish, like carp or tench, are more tolerant, particularly of the higher ranges.

Recently, in various parts of the world, acid rain has become a serious environmental problem, with the pH of some waters being lowered so much that they can no longer sustain fish life. The commonly used term 'acid rain' refers to precipitation (in the form of rain, hail or snow) which results after sulphur and nitrogen have reacted chemically with moisture in the atmosphere. Sulphur is emitted into the atmosphere from power stations, industrial plants and factories by the burning of fossil fuels, such as coal. Metal smelting works are especially noted for causing atmospheric pollution, because certain ores contain high amounts of sulphur. Large quantities of nitrogen oxides are also discharged by motor vehicles in exhaust fumes. These two chemicals, sulphur and nitrogen, are converted into sulphuric acid and nitric acid respectively by a natural process called oxidation. In addition, acid rain often contains other airborne pollutants, such as lead or mercury, which cause extra contamination problems. North America has been particularly badly affected and there are large areas where the pH of waters in rivers and lakes has become so low that they are now fishless. A number of rivers in Nova Scotia have lost all their salmon because the waters have dropped below pH5. Even though the adult fish can withstand such a low level, after spawning the resulting eggs and fry cannot tolerate it and so die. With no young fish leaving the rivers there are no adults to return and, therefore, the population disappears through lack of replacement.

In Scandinavia the Sorlandet region of Norway has lost all fish in seven major salmon rivers and it is possible that in excess of one thousand inland lakes are now fishless. In the years 1920, 1922, 1925, 1948 and 1969 major mortalities of salmon occurred in the affected rivers after heavy rain and rapid snow melt. Various suggestions were put forward at the time as to the cause of these mortalities, the favourite theory being that they were caused by toxic substances leaching from bogs. Later it was discovered that the problem was due to acid rain and had been growing progressively worse since the turn of the century.

Not only is acid rain causing losses of fish populations but it is also suspected of causing reduced forestry and crop production, damage to buildings and monuments, to human and animal health and it is even thought to be responsible for much of the corrosion to motor vehicle bodywork.

In the British Isles the prevailing winds are westerly off the Altantic and there are no industrial areas to the near west. Even so, there is evidence that some rivers and lakes on the west coasts are experiencing a slow drop in their pH values.

Suspended solids and water velocity Sea trout dislike muddy waters with high suspended solids. It has been suggested that this is why there are no sea trout runs into the Usk, Wye or Severn. Rivers like the Towy and Taf, however, have very muddy estuaries at times, but both are excellent sea trout rivers with high populations. Perhaps they move quickly through such estuarine waters to the clearer water above. What is certain is that they like the shorter, cleaner, fast-flowing rivers which most of the sea trout rivers are. Good sea trout rivers are clean, free from pollution, fast-flowing and rarely carry any amount of suspended solids, except in times of spate. They run fast, keeping gravel reaches free of weed and clear of sand and mud—areas that are essential for spawning and for the subsequent life of the young fry and parr which feed on the aquatic insects among the stones and so become fit and healthy to meet the rigorous life ahead.

These rivers also run cool, even in summer, and the turbulent nature of their course serves to oxygenate the water, which is essential to the fish's well-being.

Slower moving rivers of lowland areas have muddy bottoms with large weed beds. Temperatures can rise considerably in the summer months and the amount of dissolved oxygen can drop to low levels. Such rivers have their own adapted fish species, like carp, bream and roach.

2
Distribution

The brown trout is indigenous to most of Europe, north-western Asia, and some small areas of North Africa. In addition to these native populations they have been introduced to many parts of the world including North and South America, India and Australia. In some of these areas there have been records of migrations to the sea but no sea trout runs have established themselves to any great extent.

Sea trout are present in the coastal waters (and adjoining rivers) of northern and western Europe, from the coast of Russia to the Bay of Biscay. Notable areas are Scandinavia, Iceland and the British Isles. There are no known present populations of sea trout in the Mediterranean, although many brown trout are present in some of the countries bordering that sea. There are forms of sea trout present in the Caspian Sea and the Aral Sea but they are not quite the same fish as the northern European strain.

In 1957 I caught a small sea trout of 6 oz while angling off the northern coast of Egypt. It is possible that this fish was a stray from the Black Sea where a sub-species of *Salmo trutta* is also known to exist.

Brown trout have been introduced and are now widespread on the Atlantic seaboard of North America. The sea trout of this area, however, are not *Salmo trutta* but migratory forms of *Salvelinus fontinalis*, the American brook trout. The brook trout are very common and plentiful even in the smallest of streams, as brown trout are in the British Isles.

On the Pacific coast of North America there is yet another form of sea trout, the steelhead, which is the migratory form of the rainbow trout of that area. The rainbow trout is not native to Europe but is an introduced species.

Wherever the dominant species of trout is present in fresh waters it sustains a sea run equivalent and it seems that no other section of the salmonid family can break the stranglehold. In Europe the brown trout becomes a sea trout; in eastern North America the brook trout becomes a sea trout; and in western North America the rainbow trout becomes a sea trout or steelhead. In each case the sea run form grows to a much larger size than its fresh water counterpart.

The European sea trout is split up into different families. Unlike salmon, which as a general rule return to their river of birth, sea trout tend to stray more; although many may return to their parent stream, others may make use of several rivers, all in the same locality.

The very large sea trout of Sweden, Norway and the Baltic have possibly evolved as such to ascend the rushing mountain torrents of the region and thereby to reach their spawning grounds. The feeding grounds in the Baltic abound in sprats and shrimps which also account for fast and vigorous growth to a large size—a sea trout of 28 lb was caught on a fly in Sweden's river Em in 1930.

Normal range of sea trout on the coasts of Europe

British Populations

The sea trout of eastern Scotland are said to be a race apart from those on the western side. There is a small group of very large fish that appears in south-east England, from the Wash to the upper English Channel, which is possibly related in some way to the Scandinavian race. The east coast group is smaller (notably the Yorkshire Esk), with fewer large fish appearing, although they are still of a good average size.

The Yorkshire Esk is an excellent sea trout river and is almost in isolation on England's east coast. The rod catch is not high but commercial netsmen off the coast catch many sea trout in the 2–5 lb class, and

Key
1 Meon
2 Arun
3 Adur
4 Ouse
5 Cuckmere
6 Rother

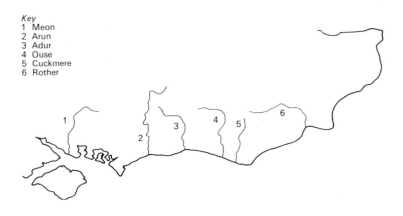

The rivers of south-east England containing sea trout

Key
1 Camel
2 Fowey
3 Looe
4 Lynher
5 Tamar
6 Tavy
7 Plym
8 Yealm
9 Erme
10 Avon
11 Dart
12 Teign
13 Exe
14 Otter
15 Axe
16 Torridge
17 Taw
18 Lyn

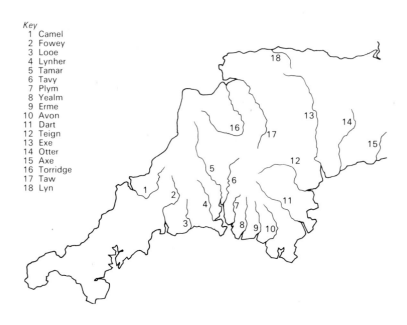

The sea trout rivers of south-west England

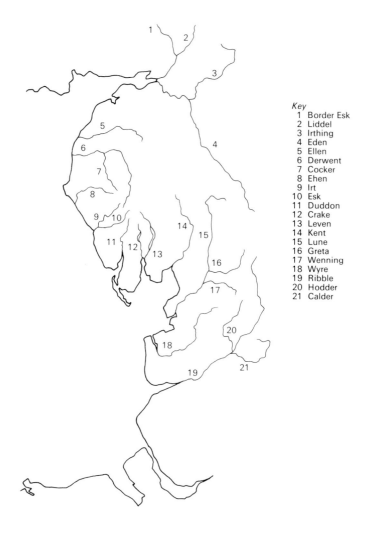

Key
1 Border Esk
2 Liddel
3 Irthing
4 Eden
5 Ellen
6 Derwent
7 Cocker
8 Ehen
9 Irt
10 Esk
11 Duddon
12 Crake
13 Leven
14 Kent
15 Lune
16 Greta
17 Wenning
18 Wyre
19 Ribble
20 Hodder
21 Calder

The sea trout rivers of north-west England

occasionally extremely large fish weighing up to 20 lb are caught (a T net off the north Yorkshire coast caught a sea trout of 22 lb in 1982). These sea trout caught by the nets off the coast are not necessarily Esk fish but may be fish travelling up the coast to more northerly rivers. There is a large commercial net fishery off the Northumberland coast which catches mainly salmon, but also a large number of sea trout, and it is known that nearly all these fish are destined for rivers in Scotland.

Table 2: Annual catches of sea trout and salmon (declared) by rods in the Yorkshire Esk, averaged over four-year periods. The resilience of sea trout stocks shows little decline over the 25 years. During the same period the salmon catch has declined markedly.

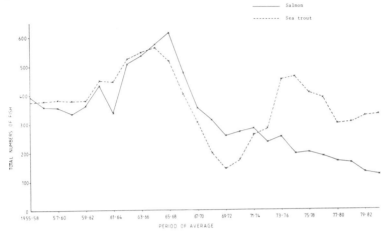

Table 3: A sample of declared catches of sea trout in Northumbria by rods and nets from 1976 to 1982.

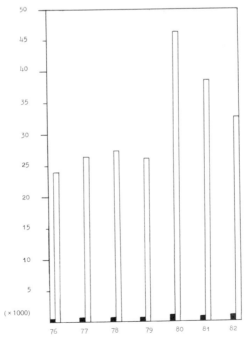

There have been reports in the past of very large sea trout being caught in the Tweed, the so-called 'bull trout' of that area. I was fortunate enough to be given the opportunity to examine sets of scales from six such fish in 1971. Although they were presented as being scales from sea trout of from 16 to 24 lb in weight, they were, in my opinion, undoubtedly salmon. The name 'bull trout' arose from the physical appearance of these fish, which are dark in colour and have many large spots on their flanks. They are probably stale salmon that have been hanging around in the estuary for a long time, or else they are spawned fish that have returned once more from the sea but have not completely lost their darkened river coats. None of the scales I examined showed more than one spawning mark and normally sea trout of this size would have spawned many times.

Key
1 Clwyd
2 Elwy
3 Conway
4 Ogwen
5 Cefni
6 Dwyfawr
7 Glaslyn
8 Mawddach
9 Wnion
10 Dysynni
11 Dovey
12 Rheidol
13 Ystwyth
14 Aeron
15 Teifi
16 Nevern
17 Western Cleddau
18 Eastern Cleddau
19 Taf
20 Gwili
21 Cothi
22 Towy
23 Gwendraeth Fach
24 Gwendraeth Fawr
25 Tawe
26 Neath

The sewin rivers of Wales

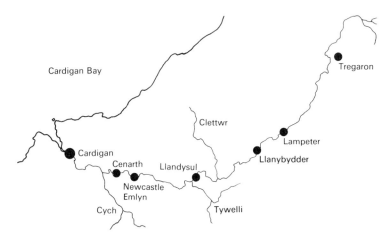

The river Teifi and its tributaries

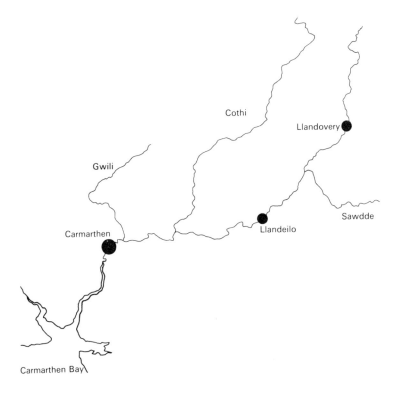

The river Towy and its tributaries

The author's largest sea trout of 12 lb 4 oz from the river Taf in 1972.

In Wales there are three distinct races of sea trout, identifiable mostly by size, which probably reflect the different feeding regimes available off the Welsh coasts. In south Wales, most notably the rivers Towy and Taf and their tributaries, the sea trout have a high average size, there being relatively few whitling and most of the fish returning after one or so years at sea, with a weight of 2 lb or more. (The river Taf is in old Pembrokeshire and is not to be confused with the Taff in Glamorgan, which lends its name to all Welshmen outside Wales!) Large multiple spawners of 5 and 6 lb are fairly common and double-figure fish occur at quite regular intervals. The largest sea trout I have caught was one of 12 lb 4 oz in the river Taf, on a spinner, on 7 July 1972. The large size of fish in this area is undoubtedly a result of the good feeding in Carmarthen Bay, a large estuarine sandy area where shellfish, shrimps and sand eels are abundant. The second family occurs off north Pembrokeshire and in southern Cardigan Bay where the rivers Nevern, Gwaun, Teifi, Aeron and Arth flow into the sea. Here, there is a very high percentage of whitling—fish that return to the rivers later in the same year they left as smolts after only four or five months feeding in the sea (so there is little sea growth). Such fish average 12 oz and range from 6 oz up to 1 lb. During some summers these shoal sewin, or sewin bach as they are called locally, ascend the rivers in thousands. The larger fish are not so numerous and double-figure fish are rare. The harsh, rocky and deep-watered unproductive coastline in this area results in less available food and slower growing, smaller fish.

A similar situation occurs on the west coast of Ireland, particularly in the counties of Mayo and Galway, where many whitling, or white trout as the sea trout is known in Ireland, return to the rivers at no more than 5 or 6 oz in weight—not a great deal larger than when they migrated to the sea a few months previously. Many do not spawn until they have migrated to the sea once more and returned to the river the following year, still barely over 1 lb in weight. A 4 lb sea trout is a good specimen for this area and double-figure fish are so rare as to be almost unknown. In Ireland sea trout of a larger size are found on the more sheltered east coast where they possibly mix with those of Welsh rivers.

The third distinct race of sea trout are those of north Wales, from the Rheidol to the Conway. There are many large fish as, again, the feeding in

Table 4: A sample of declared catches of sea trout in Wales by rods and nets from 1976 to 1982.

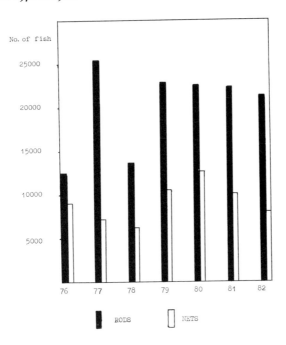

Table 5: A sample of annual Scottish sea trout catches.

	ROD AND LINE			NETS			FIXED ENGINES		
	No.	Wt lb	Avge	No.	Wt lb	Avge	No.	Wt lb	Avge
1970	38808	64755	1.67 lb	93244	239861	2.57 lb	27593	57846	2.10 lb
1971	40127	67973	1.69 lb	86473	222345	2.57 lb	31332	69377	2.21 lb

the shallower seas of north Cardigan Bay and off the north Wales coast improves the growth rate. They do not reach the same average weights of the Towy, however, which probably provides some of the best sea trout fishing in the British Isles.

STR-C

In the more prolific sea trout areas of Scotland and the Northern Isles, the west of Ireland and most of Wales the sea trout will enter the very smallest of streams to spawn. Even small brooks of just a few miles in length seem to attract them. If brown trout are present, which means that the stream does not dry up in summer, then the sea trout will also use it.

Although most prolific where they do occur, for some reason sea trout will not use certain rivers, even when the conditions would appear to be suitable. For example, there are no runs of any consequence in the Usk, Wye or Severn. That they prefer small rivers is undeniable, but the Towy is as big as the Usk and flows through similar terrain. The Vistula in Poland is a very large river and famous for its sea trout. It has been suggested that sea trout do not like muddy estuaries, but some rivers which support them have very muddy estuarine reaches. It is also strange that rivers like the Thames and Trent had prolific runs of salmon a couple of centuries ago but there is little mention in the history books of them ever having contained sea trout. Perhaps those that were present were classed as salmon. As little as thirty years ago most fish which were silver and streamlined that were caught in some Welsh rivers were called salmon, regardless of size.

In Wales the big three rivers, Towy, Teifi and Dovey, account for almost half of the sea trout caught on rod and line. Nearly every year large fish weighing up to 16 lb are caught in these rivers, with the possible exception of the Teifi where a sea trout of 10 lb or more is an infrequent occurrence. This river makes up in quantity what it may lack in quality, however, for though there is a good run of 3 to 5 lb fish early in the year, in July and August the whitling enter in thousands, giving sport to many grateful anglers. Commercial netsmen on all three of these rivers catch many sea trout in the lower tidal reaches. They are mostly fish of 3 to 6 lb, but each season usually provides catches of up to and sometimes over 20 lb. It is often said that these large fish are more likely to be salmon, but in the netsmen's case this is not very probable for they are mostly very experienced in differentiating between the two species.

Several smaller rivers in the principality yield amazing catches in some years. The Aeron in Dyfed consistently produces annual rod catches in the region of two thousand fish and surpasses three thousand in a good year, mostly whitling but with a fair sprinkling of larger fish up to 6 lb. A sea trout of 11 lb was caught in this small river in 1983 but that was an exceptionally large fish for such a small stream. Phenomenal numbers enter the river Ystwyth in years when the conditions are right during July and August. However, the river still occasionally suffers from pollution from the old lead mines, and only a couple of decades ago it was totally devoid of fish.

The Rheidol not very long ago was also so badly polluted from lead mine workings that no fish could live in it, but now it is a prime sea trout river. It has good runs of both whitling and larger fish: fish of 8 to 10 lb are caught each year, with the odd even larger one turning up. This may

Table 6: Declared catches of sea trout in the South West Water
Authority area by rods and nets from 1973 to 1982.

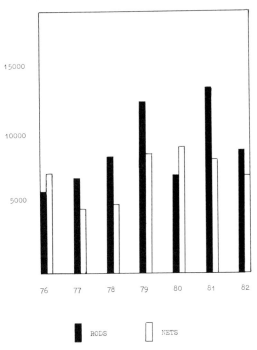

Table 7: A typical annual sample of Welsh sea trout catches (declared)
by rods and nets. (Towy figures include the rivers Gwili and Cothi.)
Those returns which showed no details of fish weights are not included.

| | RODS | | | NETS | | |
	No.	Wt lb	Avge	No.	Wt lb	Avge
TOWY	4685	13045	2.78 lb	3100	10455	3.36 lb
TEIFI	2216	3464	1.56 lb	950	3484	3.67 lb
DOVEY	2193	5781	2.63 lb	1577	5934	3.76 lb
CONWAY	378	883	2.34 lb	60	180	3.00 lb
CLWYD	717	1191	1.66 lb	1892	7403	3.91 lb

be because the Rheidol is on the border of the two races of sea trout, the northern Cardigan Bay, large Dovey population and the smaller race to the south.

Similar large runs enter the smaller rivers of north Wales at times of summer spates. The annual rod catches in good years exceed a thousand fish each in rivers such as Dwyfawr, Glaslyn Mawddach, Wnion and Seiont.

The Cumberland coast has its share also. The Lune, though famous for its salmon, provides excellent sea trout fishing, as do the smaller rivers of the area, like Duddon, Esk and Irt.

Catches

In Wales the average declared annual catch of rod-caught sea trout taken from licence returns is in the order of 22,000 fish and that for the commercial nets, 10,000 fish. The value of fish caught by commercial fishermen is much higher, for the rod catch includes a large percentage of whitling whereas the net-caught fish average over 3 lb.

The actual catch is unknown, due to the number of sea trout caught not being declared, but it is probably double that quoted and possibly even higher. If the rod catch is in the order of 40,000 fish with an average weight each of 2 lb and the commercial catch 25,000 fish of an average 3 lb, then the rivers of Wales produce something like 70 tons of sea trout per year. It is only when such figures are worked out that the extent and importance of the sea trout fisheries are truly realised. The revenue to the principality in tourism and related expenditure such as tackle, shop and hotel trade is enormous and amounts to several millions of pounds each year. A national angling survey in 1980 estimated that game anglers spent an average of over £9 for each fishing trip.

The number of anglers who send returns of their catch to the Water Authorities at the end of each season is less than fifty per cent, even though there is a legal obligation to do so. Many anglers feel that to send a true return would result in an increase in pressure on their fishing if the results were published. The returns themselves are confidential, however, and individual catches are not disclosed. The management of the resource would be better carried out if true and complete information was available to the authorities relating to the performance of the fisheries under their control.

The salmon fisheries of Wales also, of course, provide sport of some consequence, but if the Wye (which accounts for almost half the salmon rod catch) is excluded, the sea trout fisheries are of equal importance in the major rivers and more important in the numbers of smaller rivers.

In Ireland the annual total catch, both rod and commercial, ranges between 20,000 and 30,000 sea trout. The Irish figures are somewhat more realistic as the numbers are based on the estimates of the fisheries' officers in each area and not on licence returns. However, any catch statistics based on observers' estimates must be fallible, to a certain extent, and the actual catch will be higher. The counties of Connemara, Kerry, Limerick and Cork provide more than half the Irish catch. The average weight of fish caught by the rods is just 1 lb and that of the commercial fisheries $2\frac{1}{2}$ lb. It is interesting to note that the draft or seine net fish caught in estuaries or river mouths average under 2 lb but the drift net fisheries off the coast catch fish averaging over 3 lb. The fish caught at sea are possibly mixed with those destined for the Welsh or south-west English coast which are of a higher average size than the Irish native fish.

Minimum net mesh sizes operate for commercial nets all round the British Isles and no whitling are caught, as they are easily able to slip through the minimum size of mesh allowed.

The Scottish commercial catch of sea trout fluctuates between 150 and 300,000 fish per annum. The annual catch in the Tweed is between 15 and 20,000, all fish being caught in gear primarily set for salmon, as is the case in most parts of the British Isles where the sea trout commercial catch is usually incidental to that of salmon. Although the commercial catch on the Tweed is great, it is odd that this large river with its many tributaries provides little sport for sea trout anglers and the rod catch, by comparison, is very low.

Sea trout are also an important fish commercially in Iceland, Poland, Norway and Sweden.

Table 8: Average weight of sea trout for length.

Inches	lb	oz	Inches	lb	oz
8	0	5	21	4	4
9	0	6	22	4	12
10	0	8	23	5	6
11	0	10	24	6	2
12	0	13	25	6	15
13	1	0	26	7	12
14	1	4	27	8	12
15	1	8	28	9	14
16	1	15	29	11	0
17	2	5	30	12	3
18	2	12	31	13	7
19	3	4	32	14	12
20	3	12	33	16	4

3
The Life History

A great deal has been written in the past about the life history of salmon in British rivers. Most of these works give a brief description of the life style of the sea trout or offhandedly state that their habits are very similar, the only real difference being that the sea trout is a smaller fish. It is true to say that they are very similar in appearance, in fact so much alike that to many only the size is an indication of the species. They both spend a period of their lives feeding in the sea and they both return to fresh water to spawn. Having pointed out these similarities, however, there it ends. The remainder of the sea trout's life style is very different from that of the salmon and in some instances it is the complete opposite. Salmon will not take an angler's lure after dark, but for sea trout it is the most productive time. Salmon never feed in fresh water, whereas sea trout sometimes do. After spawning, sea trout generally return immediately to the sea, but salmon sometimes hang around for months. These are just a few of the differences, and as this work is concerned with sea trout their life history will be discussed and only that of the salmon referred to when it may be necessary to avoid confusion.

Adult sea trout spawn in redds, which are nests in the gravel ('beds' in Wales, 'pits' in Ireland), in the autumn. Incubation takes place during the winter months and the eggs hatch out in the early spring. The young fry then grow progressively into fingerling and parr until they turn into smolts in the spring, usually after two or three years. As smolts they migrate to the sea. They feed there until they are ready to return to the river once more and to spawn as adult fish.

Natural Spawning

By the beginning of October the ovaries of the females and the testes of the males will be well developed as spawning time approaches. Not only will the different sexes have chosen their partners but they will have positioned themselves in the river system close to the areas where spawning will take place, either at the mouths of small tributaries or in the middle reaches of the larger tributaries. When the time arrives they are then only left with a short journey to their chosen spawning area. By the end of October the females will already have made sorties upstream to explore likely gravel areas (usually called fords) and then dropped back to wait in deeper water.

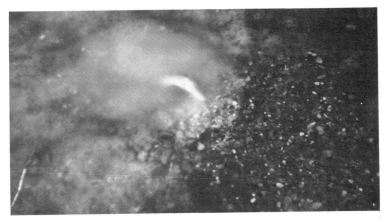

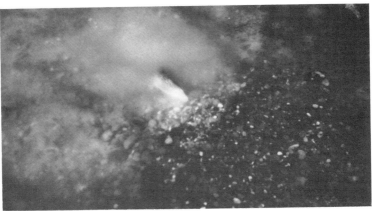

A female sea trout vigorously cutting her redd

The climate in the British Isles is such that at this time of the year it is usually wet, and the streams and tributaries are full of water when only a couple of months before there was a mere trickle. It is very rare for the rains not to come before the end of October; I can only remember one year, 1969, when most of the spawning took place in the lower reaches of the main rivers because the first flood did not arrive until the middle of November.

Many of the smaller streams that are used for spawning are almost dry during the summer, but sea trout will sometimes still spawn in the most unlikely places. I once saw a pair of whitling spawning in the gravel run-off from a farm yard, and roadside ditches that contain the necessary gravel have been used on occasion.

In south-west Wales spawning begins within a couple of days either side of 24 October. To be so precise would appear to be rather dogmatic, but it is true to say that in certain tributaries of main rivers redds appear in the

same area at roughly the same time year after year, providing that the
water conditions are right (i.e. that there is enough water). The temperature must have some governing influence; however, although it is
normally dropping at this time of year, it must be much colder in some
years than in others. It would appear, therefore, that day length is the
major factor which triggers off the spawning instinct. Fishery bailiffs and
wardens who know an area well can usually find redds in a particular
tributary at a known time, to within a day or so, each year. This time will,
of course, vary over different parts of the country.

By 5 November spawning is usually in full swing, with the bulk of the
population either in the act or just about to spawn. By mid-November
much of the spawning activity is over and is tailing off; by the end of
November, which is late in some areas, it will have finished altogether.
Spawning activity is rarely carried over into December in the south of the
country and to see any redd cutting after this date is rare. I did once
observe a pair of large sea trout spawning in a Pembrokeshire river on
Christmas Eve, but it was by far the latest effort I have ever seen. Most sea
trout have already returned to the sea by then.

Spawning site The favourite spawning site is one where the flow is fairly
fast over gravel, averaging just under an inch in diameter, in one foot of
water. Pool tails are popular areas and so are shallow runs. The fish seem
to know if the gravel is unstable and likely to shift in floods, and they will
avoid such areas even though they look perfect in every other respect.
Large fish will choose deeper water with larger gravel, possibly in the main
river or larger tributaries, and the small fish will spawn in very small
watercourses. Generally, however, the bulk of spawning will take place in
tributaries which are a few miles in length and up to ten or twelve feet
wide. In typical sea trout country such waters are pollution-free, fast-
flowing and high in dissolved oxygen.

Once the female has chosen a site, which she does by swimming slowly
over a suitable area and occasionally shuddering just over the bottom to
loosen a small amount of gravel, she will decide on a redd position and
begin in earnest.

Turning over on her side, facing upstream, the body is arched from side
to side in a vigorous swimming motion. The pectorals (the first set of
paired fins) are fully extended to act as a brake and prevent forward
motion. As a result, the gravel is loosened and forced backwards. The
stronger the flow, the more assistance it gives to the downstream movement of the gravel. When choosing the site the female has weighed up the
advantages and disadvantages—the faster the current, the easier it is to dig
the redd, but at the same time it is more difficult to work and swim against
and it requires more energy. The cutting spasm lasts only three or four
seconds and then a rest period takes place. At first the rest period amounts
to just a minute or two but as the work progresses the intervals between
cutting activity lengthen. The redd cutting is carried out either in the day
or at night; most cutting in the day is undertaken when the water is

Male and female whitling in the act of spawning, with another
curious male moving in to investigate

coloured. The period of most activity is at dusk and just after dark. Sometimes the fish will take a prolonged rest of several hours before completing the redd but, once begun, the process usually continues until the job is done. This normally takes between two and three hours. When the female has finished cutting to her satisfaction the redd can easily be seen as a hole in the gravel, six or eight inches deep, below the level of the river bed and with a mound of excavated gravel on the downstream side. Very often redds can be easily spotted, even in coloured water or poor light, for the freshly excavated gravel has a lighter appearance than its immediate surround. In the hole will be seen three or four larger stones of unequal shape resting on the bottom. At one time it was thought that the fish somehow selected these larger stones and placed them in the redd. That is not quite the case. In selecting the area for the redd the female will have chosen an area of gravel which has a few larger stones among it, as most areas of gravel do anyway. As the nest is excavated the larger stones are more difficult to remove and, therefore, collect in the depression. The sand and smaller particles of gravel wash away with the current. The unequal stones lying together have pockets in between and under them. While the redd cutting is going on another very important process is taking place in that the mud and sand are being washed out of the stones. This ensures a free flow of well oxygenated water through the redd on its completion, with much less likelihood of the eggs being smothered and dying from suffocation. Very often at each cutting spasm a puff of muddy water is seen to drift downstream.

Egg laying The female uses her anal fin to feel the nest and the shape and position of the stones at the bottom. When she is ready to begin laying her eggs the male fish, who has been standing at a distance during all the work, approaches to her side. Both fish crouch in unison, with vents pushed well down into the depression, and adopt a characteristic open-mouthed posture. Eggs are extruded by the female, several hundred at a time, and simultaneously the male ejaculates a cloud of sperm into the water. Millions of sperm are ejected, which ensures that some spermatozoa come into contact with each egg, one then entering through a small hole called the micropile, on the egg's surface, and fertilising it. The eggs sink down between the stones at the bottom of the redd. It would seem likely that the eggs would wash away downstream but they are denser than the water, and the current configuration around the hole actually draws them to the bottom. This can easily be demonstrated by digging a small hole in some gravel with a boot heel: the mud and fine particles wash away but the smaller, heavier contents tend to settle in the depression.

Immediately a particular batch of eggs has been laid and fertilised, the male swims away once more. The female then moves to the upstream edge of the hole and carries out a rigorous cutting movement which causes some gravel to fall back into the depression and completely cover the eggs. This cut is a preliminary to another round in the cycle and the process continues until all the eggs are laid and fertilised in a period ranging from fifteen minutes for small fish to several hours for large ones. Small whitling sometimes lay as few as four hundred or so eggs, while larger fish may lay as many as ten thousand. If disturbed, or if the gravel area is used up or is somehow unsatisfactory, the female may move on to another site or may rest up for twenty-four hours or more before releasing the remainder of her eggs.

Communal redds Sea trout, particularly whitling, often construct a communal redd and three or four females, together with attendant males, will use the same large redd. One male may fertilise the eggs from more than one female, for although the female is 'finished' when all her eggs have been shed the males are able to supply sperm over an extended period of several days or even weeks. The communal redd may be a type of natural insurance policy: since the redd is bigger, the eggs will be safer and there will be less silt and better water circulation. It may also mean that the weaker females who possibly cannot dig their own redd are able to spawn in redds made for them by stronger fish. Another reason for communal redds is that, as in south Wales, for instance, there may be a shortage of males, with the females outnumbering them by perhaps three to one. In such cases it is obviously necessary for more than one female to spawn together to ensure the attendance of a male fish. If they spawned separately there would not be enough male fish to service all the females. In south Wales the salmon do not have such a problem; in fact, the situation in reverse is common—in the Towy in particular there are as many as four male salmon to every female.

When the redd is complete, the female, spent, drops downstream and as soon as she has recovered sufficiently starts the journey down to the sea. The males may linger around the redd area for a few hours just in case another female arrives ready to spawn. At this time salmon males become very aggressive and will rush about, chasing small brown trout away and even seizing floating leaves as they pass by. I have never seen this behaviour among sea trout, although it is common among brown trout. By Christmas the majority of the sea trout kelts (spawned fish) have returned to the sea.

The first flush of water after the redd has been completed serves to fill in any remaining depression with gravel and smooth over the surface. There is a danger in the first few days that a heavy flood may wash away the already loosened gravel if the bed is at all unstable, but once the gravel has settled and become somewhat compacted the eggs are safe. The pockets left between the stones which contain the clusters of eggs are well supplied with oxygenated water continually percolating through the gravel.

Artificial Spawning

When the female is ripe for spawning the membrane, or roe sac, containing the eggs ruptures and the eggs separate and fall loose within the body cavity. This process takes about twenty-four hours, the eggs nearest the vent separating first and those at the front of the body last. At this time the eggs will be at their optimum potential of fertility. If spawning is delayed for some reason then they will deteriorate over a period of time until after about a week if the eggs are not shed they are unlikely to be any good whatsoever. Fish that do not spawn, possibly due to the lack of suitable gravel or the absence of a mate, may reabsorb the eggs, may shed them in an unsuitable place, resulting in a total loss, or may die spawnbound.

If a ripe fish is held up tail downwards, the force of gravity alone will cause some eggs to drop from the vent. They can at this time be squeezed gently from the fish into a bowl or other receptacle, a process known as stripping. When the eggs are first extruded they are soft and flaccid and of unequal shape. On the surface of each egg there is a minute hole called the micropile. Milt from a male fish stripped in a similar fashion must be mixed with the eggs to enable a sperm to find the micropile, enter the egg and fuse with the nucleus, so fertilising it. In the river the sperm is washed away almost immediately. Just a teaspoonful contains millions of individual sperm, which swim by lashing their long tails, and this ensures that in the couple of seconds available to them one sperm is sure to come into contact with an egg to fertilise it. As soon as the eggs are laid they begin to absorb water and swell, which causes the micropile to close, so any egg not fertilised almost immediately will remain infertile and no amount of contact from sperm later will affect it.

Hatchery workers strip the eggs into a bowl containing no water so that the micropiles will remain open longer. Fertilisation rates can be very good if the operation is carried out correctly and with care. Spermatozoa can live in water for only about thirty seconds but are able to live much longer in ovarian fluid (a small amount of body fluid which the female extrudes with the eggs), so the dry method of stripping also enables the sperm to live longer and increases the chances of all the eggs being fertilised. However, there are several dangers to guard against when spawning fish artificially.

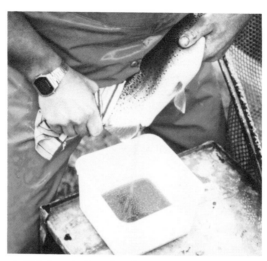

Artificially stripping a female

The milt is used to fertilize the eggs

Eyed eggs and newly hatched alevins

Thousands of young trout fry in a hatchery tank

Bright sunlight will kill eggs, as will any dramatic change in temperature. It is also important to exclude any foreign matter like slime, blood, faeces, broken eggs or dirt, as any of these will make it more difficult for the sperm to find the micropile which may be blocked by them. Broken eggs release the sticky albumen and are a common cause of poor fertilisation. They are usually the result of using too much pressure when stripping a fish that is not quite ripe.

After stripping, the eggs harden off over a period of about half an hour, absorbing water until firm and round. They vary a little in size according to the size of the parent, but average about three-sixteenths of an inch in diameter. After hardening they are placed in specially constructed trays that ensure an even flow of water over them, and are kept in the dark to simulate the natural undergravel conditions of a redd.

Early Development

The development of the incubating eggs is dependent on temperature. The colder the water, the longer they take to hatch, and in severe weather, when the temperature of the water is just above freezing, there is little progress at all. If the eggs should freeze they will die. There are several other dangers to the redd: there is the chance, already mentioned, of heavy floods washing the gravel away; there is also the possibility of low water conditions, which could leave the redd high and dry. It has been suggested that the eggs will die if the redd is exposed but this is not always the case for, even though the surface of the gravel may become dry, there could still be some flow underneath, enabling the eggs to survive for some consider-able time as long as they remain moist. The worst danger to drying-out redds is freezing, since drought during the winter is usually accompanied by sub-zero temperatures.

It was thought at one time that the redds were subject to predation by eels, but this has now been discounted as extremely unlikely. Although larger invertebrates in the gravel would eat eggs, it is doubtful whether they would be actively feeding at this time of the year.

By far the biggest cause of mortality among incubating eggs is the spread of fungus. This organism will attack any dead, infertile or damaged eggs and will then spread to other live eggs lying adjacent to them. The danger is well known to hatchery keepers, and incubating eggs in the hatchery are regularly treated with the fungicide, Malachite Green, to prevent this kind of infection.

Sea trout eggs will hatch in about forty-two days at 10°C (50°F), but will take over one hundred and fifty days to hatch at 1°C (34°F). From this it can be deduced that in southern Britain incubation times are reasonably rapid, whereas in northern Scotland and Scandinavia, for example, the eggs take much longer to develop. The reason is that newly hatched fry are dependent on micro-organisms in the water to feed on in the spring. Cold water inhibits the development of this food supply which is essential to the

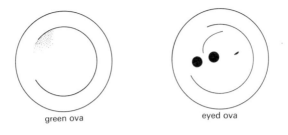

green ova   eyed ova

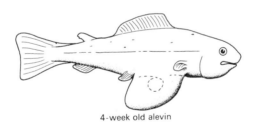

newly hatched alevin

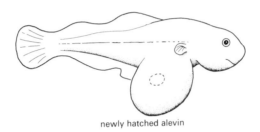

4-week old alevin

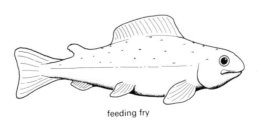

feeding fry

Early stages of development in the sea trout

fish in the early stages, and so the fish hatch out to coincide with the warming spring weather.

Shortly after being laid, the eggs become very delicate and any disturbance will kill them. About half way through the incubation period they become 'eyed' and much hardier, and are less susceptible to shock. The term 'eyed' ova means that the eyes of the developing embryo inside the egg can be seen clearly as two black dots. These are the first pigment to develop.

Hatching When hatching time approaches, the alevin (as it is called when it first hatches) secretes an enzyme which softens the eggshell and makes it relatively easy to break through. Looking very unlike an actual fish, the alevins have a large yolk sac attached to the stomach. They are quite transparent at this stage and on close examination with the naked eye the heart can be seen beating. They remain in the pockets beneath the gravel safe from harm for a further five to six weeks, depending again on the temperature. The yolk sac is gradually absorbed, providing the only sustenance during this period.

As the yolk sac is on the point of disappearing the most critical stage approaches and the young fry must emerge from the confines of the gravel and seek food for the first time. The young fish will drift downstream with the current until it finds a suitable location in a patch of slacker water where it can seize any small organisms as they drift by. Mortality at this time is tremendously high: many fry are taken by willing predators, such as other fish (even their own kind) and many species of birds. Considerable numbers will also fail to find enough food to sustain them and will quickly become emaciated and die.

In hatcheries this is also a critical time. The young fry must be fed a finely crumbed, specially prepared diet at frequent intervals throughout the day so that as many as possible will come on to the feed. Modern dry-feed diets, high in the necessary proteins, have now been developed for the difficult early feeding period. A few years ago the only successful method of getting young fry to feed was to offer them very finely minced, raw beef liver as a starter diet and later to wean them off this on to a dry pelleted food.

In the wild some researchers have concluded that as many as 95 per cent of the young fry die in the first three months after hatching. In the protected environment of a hatchery mortality rates are much lower.

Life in the River

The young fry soon become territorial in their behaviour; that is, they take up a station in a quiet eddy of the stream, either in front of or behind a stone or other shelter, and chase any intruders away from their domain. They are constantly on the alert for food and dart out into the faster current to seize likely morsels that pass by. For the first three or four months they are known as fingerlings, and as they grow larger they gradually develop the distinctive parr markings on the flanks, like a row of finger prints. As they become fitter and stronger those that were hatched out high up in small tributaries will gradually make their way downstream to deeper, more secure territories. Lower down, the food supplies will be more plentiful as summer approaches and some of the areas, which provided refuge when the rivers were swollen with the winter rain, will be turning to mere trickles in the drier weather. There are only two necessary functions of life to concern them at this time—one, to stay alive and the other, to search constantly for food.

Through the first summer the fish put on weight and grow stronger, until by the early autumn they will be about three inches long. The rate of growth will depend to a great extent on the productivity of the waters and the available food supply. Food consists of a variety of organisms. Terrestrial insects, such as the many species of flies that land on the water and beetles and caterpillars that fall off the bushes and trees, are taken avidly. However, the vast amount of water creatures, the invertebrates, probably make up the staple diet. Snails, caddis larvae and small fish fry of minnows, bullheads and stone loaches are all taken when the opportunity arises and sometimes, during flash floods and freshets, earthworms and slugs are gratefully added to the list.

In northern cold-water climates, growth will be much slower than in southern England, for example, where growth may even continue slowly throughout the winter months when food occasionally becomes available. With the onset of winter the parr will move out of the fast runs and 'stickles' where they have found their food, travel downstream into the deeper water of the pools and hide close to or under the bank, or under stones. The metabolic rate slows down considerably in the low temperatures. Food may be only rarely available and very often may not be taken even when it is.

Activity increases as the days lengthen and the water temperature rises in the spring. The surviving young parr, now one year old, lean and fit, begin feeding once more. A gradual but steady movement downstream occurs through the summer as the parr drop down from the higher tributaries into the main streams. By about August they average five inches in length and a slow change in their appearance begins to take place. Until this time they have been indistinguishable from the resident brown trout and have mixed with them, competing for food and territories, but now their appearance and habits start to alter. The scales along the sides begin to take on a silvery tint, which is due to the depositing of a substance called guanine on the scales. A marked downstream migration occurs in September, particularly during floods, and the fish begin to congregate in small shoals in the middle and lower reaches of the main river. The parr marks are now fading rapidly and on some fish have already almost disappeared; all the time the colouring is becoming lighter and more silvery. The migration to sea as a smolt is fast approaching.

Journey to the Sea

In their second winter in the river there is no resting up in the pools in a semi-torpid state. In the lower reaches of the river, even in winter, there is not a great deal of food, but even so there is considerably more than in the colder upstream tributaries and what is available is seized willingly. By the end of December the larger, faster growing fish, which may have reached a length of as much as eight inches by now, turn completely silver and leave the river for the sea. The migration has begun. Through January, February and into March it builds up to a crescendo. At this time the fish lose all their spots and parr markings and turn completely silver, apart from the characteristic yellowy-orange tip to the adipose fin which identifies them so positively with the genus, *trutta*. The shoals drop downstream mostly at night, but flood water is the favourite time and the vast majority leave the river at times of heavy water. It is undoubtedly easier for them to adapt to the change from fresh to salt water when there is more dilution because of the large volume of river water entering the sea.

Most parr that find enough food in the spring to reach a size of six inches or more will turn into smolts and enter the sea. A proportion of the later downstream arrivals, however, will be too small and will not migrate but move upstream again to gain one more summer's growth. These fish will then drop down once more in the autumn to be the first and largest to leave the following year at the beginning of the next migration cycle.

By the end of April only a few stragglers will be left and among these there will be some who just cannot make up their minds. For some reason they will hang about in the harbours or estuaries, forsaking the fresh water river life but not going to sea to seek the abundant food like the majority of their brethren. In April, and throughout May, the salmon smolt migration begins as the sea trout's ends.

The general pattern of young sea trout growth and migration varies in different localities and in different countries. In the warmer climate of France and southern England the whole cycle may be accelerated, eggs will hatch out sooner and parr will grow faster. Many smolts will migrate after only one year's growth in the river. In much colder areas of the north, such as Iceland or Scandinavia, it may be four or five years or even more before the parr reach sufficient size to warrant the beginning of their life at sea.

It is very difficult to give accurate figures of the number of sea trout smolts that migrate from particular rivers, and no doubt it varies tremendously. Some very rough back calculations can be made, however, if the number of fish caught is known. This is the only figure that can be estimated with any confidence. If the rod catch amounts to 1,000 adult fish and it is taken to be some 30 per cent of the total run, then the run of sea trout into the river is somewhere in the order of 3,300 fish. In salmon rivers 20 per cent to the rods is generally regarded as a fair estimate of the number of fish so taken. Sea trout, being more numerous and somewhat easier to catch at certain times, are more likely to yield something like 30 per cent to the rods. Survival from the smolt stage to adults is unlikely to be more than about 40 per cent, so such a river would have a smolt run in the region of 8,000. The smolts produced by any given sea trout river can, therefore, be estimated to be something like eight times the total rod catch for that river. The corresponding figures in a river that has a rod catch of about 5,000 would be 16,500 adults and 41,250 smolts. These figures are only a very rough guide, as there are numerous other factors to be considered, not least the varying ages of the returning adults, some being smolts the previous year, some the year before that, and so on.

Life in the Sea

Once the fish reach the sea the increased food supply results in a dramatic increase in growth, which can very easily be seen when examining the scales. The main diet consists of small fish, such as sprats, brett and sand eels, which move around in vast shoals in coastal waters, especially during the summer months. Sea trout do not travel far out to sea like the salmon but remain within the confines of the continental shelf. The favoured areas are the shallow productive regions of the Baltic, the North Sea and the Irish Sea. Some of the smaller fish do not venture more than a few miles from the coast and remain within the vicinity of the mouth or estuary of the parent river. This fact is illustrated by the capture of sea trout, intentionally or otherwise, in coastal nets during all months of the year. These coastal fish probably feed on a variety of crustaceans, such as shrimps and prawns, little shoaling fish, like pollack and whiting, as well as other small coastal water inhabitants, such as pouting and gobies.

Some of the larger sea trout travel considerable distances around the coasts in search of feeding grounds and these areas are well known to commercial fishermen who can make large catches at certain times of the year. Perhaps the most productive commercial sea trout fishery is along the Northumbrian coastline, though most of the fish caught are from Scottish rivers. Sea trout are caught in some numbers off the south-east coast of England, notably the Wash, although there are no sea trout rivers in that area. An important sea trout fishery occurs off the coast of Denmark, where they are also caught on rod and line in the sea, but there are very few sea trout rivers in that country.

Return to the River

A large proportion of the sea trout return to the river after only a few months feeding in the sea and are called whitling, (age classification 2.0 +). These small fish have various local names in different parts of the country—finnock, herling or peal being the most common. The names can be a little confusing: for instance, peal (small sea trout in Cornwall and the south) is also the name used for smolts, both sea trout and salmon smolts in west Wales.

It is not known why whitling decide to return to the river in the first summer after migration—the reason may be hereditary. There is no equivalent stage in salmon, the earliest return being that of grilse after 1 + years of sea growth, that is, in the second summer after migration from the river.

The run of whitling in Wales, where the fish are also referred to as shoal sewin, schoolies or sewin bach, begins with a very few fish towards the end of May, builds up slowly during June and reaches a peak by the end of July. The exact timing of the runs will vary according to the water conditions, as they generally enter the rivers in quantity during times of flood. If no floods occur, however, as sometimes happens in a dry summer, these fish will enter the river in July, even in drought conditions. The average size is 12 oz and rarely do they reach 1 lb in weight. In late July and August some of them are quite small, hardly any more than 5 or 6 oz. These are fish which left the river in late April or May, stayed close to the river mouth or remained in the estuary, and then joined in the upstream migration of the returning larger fish. Such unusually small fish will not spawn, and many of them will journey upstream for a short distance and then return to the sea.

It was once thought that whitling did not spawn at all, but the majority of them do: it is only the smaller individuals which return to the sea without maturing. In 1973 and 1974 I purposely kept over 100 whitling females, with an average weight of 10 oz, in a holding tank at a rearing station off the river Teifi. All these fish without exception produced viable eggs but this was twenty miles from the sea, so it is quite possible that any smaller immature fish do not venture so far upstream if their intentions are not towards reproduction. At one time even grilse were considered to be immature salmon and a few popular dictionaries still describe them so. They are, of course, smaller fish which mature earlier and in some salmon rivers they are the most important age class to the reproductive process.

In several areas, the west of Ireland in particular, the whitling are very small, sometimes hardly any bigger than normal smolt size, and the majority of these fish will not reach maturity until they have gone back to the sea for a further year's growth.

The first sea trout to enter the rivers are the maiden fish, returning twelve months or more after their migration as smolts. Aged 2.1 +, the scales show a full summer's sea growth plus one winter's growth. Some enter the lower reaches as early as the beginning of March but the main run occurs at the end of April and into May. These are the prettiest of fish, with deep silver bodies, very few spots and small heads, and are probably the strongest fighting fish for their weight that an angler is likely to meet anywhere. They can be much more numerous in some rivers than others; the runs of this class of sea trout in the Towy are famous among sea trout anglers.

The size of the age group ranges from $1\frac{1}{2}$ up to 4 lb, with an average of somewhere around $2\frac{1}{2}$ lb. The early run fish can be difficult to catch, especially if the water temperature is low. They do not seem to show a great deal of interest in anglers' lures until later in April or early May when the water temperatures start to rise. A run of these fish in a late May or early June flood can provide the most spectacular sport on a spinner if the conditions are good. In June, the recent fresh runners will also take a fly well at night in the lower reaches of some rivers.

The third category of fish to include here are those termed 'previous spawners'. These range from fish of just 2 lb, which spawned the previous year as whitling, to the very large multiple spawners. Once a fish has spawned, either as a whitling or a second sea-winter fish, it normally spawns each year thereafter until death. A few may miss a year in between spawning and are called 'long-absence' fish, but these are much more uncommon than the individuals which spawn every year. Sea trout that have spawned three or four times and weigh from 5 to 8 lb are fairly common on several of the larger rivers, and some of the very big fish may have spawned up to ten times (a sea trout that had spawned twelve times has been recorded). Most of the previous spawners enter the river during May and June, the latter month being when the majority of large previously spawned fish are caught by anglers.

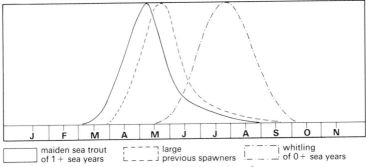

Duration and timing of sea trout runs from the sea into the rivers of west Wales.

Late runs In some of the rivers of Wales a late run of previous spawned large sea trout occurs in late September and early October. These fish are very dark in colour and are heavily spotted. They are brown, trout-like in appearance and are almost all males. Several years ago they were regarded as a different sub-species of late running sea trout and called bull trout. In Cardiganshire they are known as Brith y dail (or Brych y dail), meaning speckled or spotted leaves. Further south in Carmarthen and Pembroke they are called Twps y dail, meaning stupid leaves, possibly due to the fact that at times they are very easy to catch and will seize a spinner in a quite suicidal fashion. All sea trout in the river become darker as the season progresses, until at spawning time they have lost nearly all the silver sheen of their sea coat and turned to a much darker brown colour, with more accentuated spots. The so-called bull trout of west Wales are fish that have already begun to take on the dress of their spawning colours before they enter the river.

The homing instinct of salmon is well known and can only be described as one of the wonders of nature, particularly as they travel so far in the ocean and are then able to return to the rivers of their birth. In sea trout the homing instinct is not quite as well developed and, though many fish return to their parent river each year, there is a certain amount of straying. Very often they will return to another river in the same locality as the one of their birth. All rivers have their own chemical characteristics, according to the type of terrain through which they drain, and no doubt neighbouring rivers have similar qualities. The returning fish are able to detect the taste and smell of their own rivers. This could be the reason why many enter the rivers at times of flood. Not only does the heavier water make access easier, but it also means that the smell of the river is accentuated and the larger flow volumes entering the sea make finding it that much easier. As many sea trout do not travel far from the mouth of their home river, the homing instinct does not need to be so finely tuned. Their tendency to stray somewhat is also a useful natural safety valve to ensure the repopulation of a stream from others nearby, should a mishap occur, such as serious pollution.

4
Predation

Predation plays a major role in the life of the sea trout, for it is at all times subject to many dangers. It has evolved, as many animals have, as an efficient, strong and fast species, not only to assist it in avoiding predation but also to enable it to be a predator itself. Its swimming speed and strength are far in excess of those possessed by many other fish, and enable it to escape from predators in the clear water of the river and later from the ever present hunters in the sea. Its colouring is such that the fish is well camouflaged from both above and below. Looking up at the white belly, it is almost invisible against the sky, and from above it blends in with most backgrounds. To the inexperienced observer, spotting sea trout in quite shallow clear water is difficult, because they lie stationary, with only the fins wavering slightly to hold station. It is only when they move that they become visible. Though the adult fish are not mottled, like young parr, brown trout, pike or perch which blend in easily with a pebbled or weedy background, they still seem to have the ability to disappear into almost complete obscurity. Only when the sun is overhead and their shadows cast on the bottom are they reasonably easy to detect.

A clear indication of the amount of predation to which a species is subject can be related to the number of offspring that it produces. In effect, if the mating of one animal with another produces two offspring, one male and one female, then the level at which that species continues to exist, i.e. its total population, will remain constant (assuming that roughly two die for every two produced). This is, of course, a theoretical assumption and all sorts of fluctuations naturally occur; however, the theory does relate the number of offspring to the number that are likely to survive.

Sea trout lay, on average, seven hundred eggs for every pound of body weight, i.e. a five-pound female produces roughly three thousand five hundred eggs. A very large percentage of these must die, otherwise the species would become too numerous for the available food supply and would either starve or fall victim to disease, parasites, etc. This does actually happen to animal populations on occasions if they over-produce, and hence the culling operations carried out on some species.

Cod produce millions of eggs at spawning time to cope with the phenomenal predation of the plankton-like larvae and fry. Seagulls which have few predators produce an average of two eggs, whereas mallard, which have several predators, produce an average of twelve eggs. Animals that have no normal predators (only man), such as elephants or whales, normally produce only one or two young, and at lengthy intervals. From the moment an egg is laid to the time a sea trout spawns, it is faced with danger and is subject to many forms of predation. Once a sea trout has survived to spawn, however, the necessary act of procreation has been completed and death can then be naturally accepted, even though the fish has the ability to spawn on subsequent occasions should it survive. Atlantic salmon rarely recover to spawn for a second time (4 per cent being a general average) and only an exceptional few spawn more than twice.

It is, therefore, necessary for about two fish to survive from the average spawning of around 1400 eggs—a mortality rate of 99.86 per cent. By far the highest mortality period is in the river during the first three months or so of life when as many as 95 per cent will perish. These losses are not all the result of predation, as there are many other reasons why spawning and early life may not be successful, such as starvation, floods, drought or pollution.

Birds

Almost any bird will eat young fry if it can catch them. On a fish farm where thousands of fry were kept in shallow tanks I have seen crows, magpies, wagtails, dippers, kingfishers and herons all helping themselves at times when nobody was about. This was only because, being so concentrated in this unnatural environment, the fish were very easy to catch. Of these birds it is probable that dippers, kingfishers and herons are the only ones capable of catching fish in a stream under natural conditions. Dippers most certainly do. Their artful practice of walking under the water and searching for food in between the stones and in the moss make them well adapted to catching fry which have newly emerged from the gravel. The beautiful kingfisher is an expert underwater fisherman, too, and will catch fish up to three inches in length. These birds are not plentiful, however, and it would be heartless indeed to begrudge them their reasonable share. The dipper's main diet is underwater invertebrates, with only the occasional tiny fish being eaten when the opportunity presents itself. The kingfisher also feeds on other small insects and fish, such as minnow, bullheads and small eels.

Herons It is difficult to raise any sympathy for herons, however, and most trout fishermen dislike their presence on any form of trout fishery, because they can do a considerable amount of damage to fish stocks. They will take any size fish, from fry up to fish $1\frac{1}{2}$ lb in weight, if the occasion arises, and they can be particularly destructive on fish farms where large concentrations of fish can be taken from tanks or ponds. It is commonly believed that herons are waders only, but I have seen them alight on the water of a heavily stocked pond, seize a fish and fly off again, in a similar fashion to swallows taking insects from the water surface. They very rarely resort to this method, however, and usually play the waiting game for which they have the proverbial patience of Job. As many as twenty or thirty of these birds can raid a farm over a period of time and cause substantial economic losses, not only in numbers of fish caught but in the many fish wounded by their sharp, stabbing beaks and then dropped. Such fish are no longer any use for sale and can be the cause of disease and infections spreading among the healthy fish. The only way to deter herons completely is to have all the ponds or tanks covered with netting to prevent their entry. Even then it is surprising how this most intelligent and sly bird can gain access to its favourite dish—stew-pond trout!

The heron is not such a menace on rivers, for fish are not as plentiful or readily available and take much more skill to catch. Besides fish, herons will also eat small animals and reptiles. Frogs and newts can be the mainstay of the diet during certain months of the year, frogs being particularly vulnerable when they are spawning. Tadpoles, too, are gratefully received. If times are hard, herons will also forage in the fields for grubs and worms. They nest in heronries, which are large nests of twigs in the tops of tall trees, and there can be up to fifty nests in each colony. It is unfortunate if you are a trout fishery owner and one is close by. The adult birds sometimes have territories which may extend many miles from their heronry base.

Various species of duck are sometimes accused of eating fry in the rivers, but fry would not be a normal diet and whether they are taken in any quantity is doubtful.

Cormorants When the young fry have survived this barrage of predation and grown to a size when they are ready to turn into smolts and migrate downstream towards the sea, they meet one of the worst of their enemies, the cormorant. Smolt fishing is an annual and most productive feast for cormorants. However, only some take up the habit, possibly taught by their parents, and many more will remain on the coast. They will

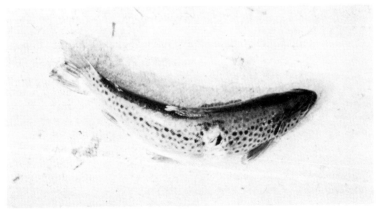

A 1 lb brown trout with a fatal heron stab

fly inland, sometimes great distances, to intercept the downstream migrating smolts in the spring and are at this time undoubtedly responsible for heavy losses of these recruits to future sea trout runs. The fishing begins in late January and sometimes lasts well into May. The cormorants especially like to rest and dry their wings, sitting in the topmost branches of tall, dead trees from which take off is easy when they are alarmed. They are the clumsiest of birds taking off from the water and need a runway of fifty yards or so to become airborne. For this reason they only fish the lower reaches of large rivers and the harbours and river mouths of the smaller streams, and are rarely seen on streams or fish farm ponds. They will occasionally raid lakes or reservoirs where they can also do much damage to stocks of trout. Fish of up to 2 lb are regularly eaten, and when feeding on smolts it takes eight to ten of them to make a decent meal. If a dozen cormorants fish a river mouth for a couple of months, the numbers of fish eaten could run into thousands. It is strange that this bird is so common on the coasts, often breeding in colonies of several thousand, and yet only a minute proportion of them adopt the smolt fishing habit. The only comments to be made in their defence are that they are also partial to eels and flounders and that they may not be feeding exclusively on smolts.

In the west of Ireland and some parts of Scotland the merganser, a type of fish-eating duck, is notorious as a smolt fisherman, and has been the subject of many surveys. It is very difficult to assess the damage caused by fish-eating birds but figures are sometimes quoted. It has been suggested that a merganser can eat over a thousand smolts per annum, so where these birds are plentiful it is possible that they are responsible for the loss of many fish that would otherwise return to the rivers as adults. I once saw a merganser shot at the mouth of a small river in Ireland. It was almost oblivious to its surroundings as it fished for smolts, continuously diving, and came within easy reach of a shotgun waiting on shore. When it was opened up it contained a mixture of sea trout and salmon smolts.

Seagulls The humble seagull, normally a scavenger, can sometimes learn to be an excellent fish-catcher. It will certainly take fish from farm ponds and the odd bird will stand poised at the side of a waterfall or rapid stretch of water waiting for a fish to make a mistake and come close to the bank within range. The artful seagulls become surprisingly quick and their strong beaks rarely allow escape once they have taken hold. Some seagulls even learn to dive from a height of several feet into the water to seize a fish. Although I have only seen herring gulls and black backs engaging in this practice, on a fish farm the fish are so easy to catch that any type of gull is attracted. They will take sea trout of up to 3 lb weight if they can manage to drag them out, but smolts or parr are the more usual catch. Some gulls also become proficient at catching eels in harbours and estuaries.

In Scotland ospreys are on the increase; however, their numbers are so small that any significant loss of fish is unlikely. They, like the heron, have discovered that fish farm ponds provide rich pickings.

On the coast and at sea little is known about predation of sea trout by birds. The fish are probably much more difficult to catch than in the confines of a river or estuary. It is possible that cormorants still catch a few but these birds feed mainly on pollack, whiting, cod and other marine species. Gannets, of which there are large concentrations in some areas, are very efficient fish-eating birds and they may catch sea trout from time to time. However, their staple diet is fish which swim in shoals near the surface, like sprats, herrings and mackerel.

Mammals

There are very few animals which rely solely on a diet of fish in the river and none, except for the otter, in Britain. There are many, however, that are grateful for any that may happen their way. Foxes, badgers, wild cats, rats and small carnivores like stoats and weasels all find fish quite acceptable. Catching live fish is another matter and probably the only time that they become available to them are when they die, are stranded (perhaps after floods), or when they are dropped or discarded by other predators, even, perhaps, left in the shade under a tree by some unfortunate angler.

Otters The one animal that can be accused of taking fish in any number is the otter, but it is by no means certain how many fish are caught by otters or what damage they do. They have long been blasted, hated and wished into extinction by some game anglers and past records have condemned them as highly undesirable. What then is the true story? Conservationists will say that they do little damage to game fisheries and that their main diet is eels. That they do catch and eat sea trout and salmon is beyond question, but as to the actual number consumed little is really known.

Otters are not plentiful (though there are far more of them than the conservationists would have us believe), and modern industry and population growth have certainly reduced their numbers to a much lower level than they once were. These days, because of their apparent scarcity, it is unlikely that they do much harm. The reason that otters have been declared so scarce is that they are rarely, if ever, seen by people. In over thirty years of fishing in the rivers of south-west Wales (at all times of the day and night) I have only actually had a good identifiable sight of an otter on about a dozen occasions. They are, of course, almost entirely nocturnal, unless disturbed, and many times I have known that they were there, or strongly sensed their presence in the dark. Between 1970 and 1977 I knew of two regularly inhabited holts on the middle reaches of the Teifi and in at least four of those years a litter of cubs was raised. Only once did I see a litter of about four animals in bright moonlight (they were never brought out in the day) but I often knew they were near and I could hear the cubs playing close by. Sometimes, while fishing the tail of a pool where one of the holts was situated, I would become aware of their presence and step silently back under a large ash tree and hope for a glimpse in the poor light. Mostly, it was splashes, boils and wakes only, for spotting an otter in the darkness was extremely difficult.

One night I had caught two nice sea trout, each of about 2 lb, and laid

them on the gravel as I moved downstream covering the pool. On my
return they had gone. I had lost fish once or twice like this before and put
it down to rats, but that night it seemed impossible that two good-sized
fish should disappear so swiftly and silently. I immediately suspected that
they had been taken by young otters, for I had sensed their presence while
fishing. The very next night I approached the river as normal and began
fishing in the usual place. On catching a fish after a few minutes, I laid it
on the gravel in the same place as before and then moved silently back
under the ash tree. After a wait of about fifteen minutes, in the gloom, I
saw an otter come to the edge of the gravel, pause and look around, then
silently leave the water, run forward and seize my fish—gone in a flash
almost before I had realised what had happened.

This, perhaps unique, incident that I had witnessed had probably been
possible because the young otters were used to my presence, as I fished
there almost every night when the conditions were right, and they knew
that I meant them no harm. I was also an easy touch for a free meal as it
turned out. Shortly after, the litter dispersed, much to my disappointment.

The question as to whether the presence of an otter spoils the fishing has
been answered for me. If the otter is hunting, yes; if he is playing or just
passing through, no. The fish seem able to sense if there is any danger,
possibly in the same way that the wildebeeste know whether a lion is lazing
and uninterested or is intent on a kill. I have caught sea trout on a fly
literally amongst the playing cubs. At other times the presence of an otter
has brought all fishing to a standstill, despite being lively previously.

Mink The mink, a relation of the otter, is now beginning to establish itself
in some parts of the country. They are not natural residents, but have
escaped from farms where they are reared for their fur. There are pockets
of mink colonies in several parts of south Wales. They are nowhere near
as efficient a fish catcher as otters, and are much smaller in size. Not only
do they eat fish but they are known to feed on any small animals or birds,
chickens being a particular favourite. Like a fox, they have a reputation for
being destructive killers, sometimes destroying far more than they can
possibly eat. Any damage caused to sea trout stocks is probably very small.

When sea trout reach the sea they are always in danger from one of
nature's most lethal of fish-eating animals, the seal. How many sea trout
and salmon they eat, as opposed to marine species of fish, is unknown but
it is possible that in some areas the former make up the major part of the
diet. The presence of large colonies of seals off Scottish coasts are thought
to make considerable inroads into game fish stocks. On the Northumberland coast they raid commercial fishermen's nets and either take or
seriously damage the fish caught in them. This not only causes the loss of
fish but expensive damage to the nets and gear as well. The seal population
is increasing all around Britain's coasts at the present time. Like cormorants after the smolts, some seals learn that lower river and estuarine
fishing can produce rich rewards.

Fish

Predatory fresh water fish, such as pike, perch and chub, rarely occur in sea trout rivers. In west Wales only the Towy contains pike and even these are relatively few in number. Such fish do not seem to do well in fast-flowing streams. There have been instances of perch and pike in the Teifi but, fortunately, they have never managed to establish themselves. These fish cannot, therefore, be considered as serious predators of sea trout, but where they do occur there is no doubt that parr and smolts or even the odd larger fish will be on the menu.

In the early stages of life the sea trout itself is probably one of its own most serious predators. Young brown trout and sea trout parr will feed on the fry and small fish of their own kind whenever they can catch them. They are very partial to eggs and there are always small fish in attendance at spawning time, lurking close by and ready to dart forwards to seize any stray eggs that do not get buried in the gravel. Some will be even bold enough to advance under the female as she lays her eggs and take one before it has sunk to the bottom of the redd. All salmonids are very keen on the eggs of their own species and salmon paste, or jam as it is sometimes known, is a noted bait for trout, though quite illegal. Whether this cured or preserved form of eggs is as good as it is made out to be, or anything like the real thing, remains open to question.

Once the young fry have absorbed the yolk sac and are emerging from the gravel they are again subject to heavy predation by their own kind and may well be eaten by their brethren of the previous year's hatch, to sustain life and promote growth for the subsequent journey down river to the sea. It can be seen from this that the term 'cannibal trout', applied by many anglers to large river trout, is really a misnomer; all trout are cannibals, given the opportunity. A six-inch trout is capable of eating a three-inch trout and probably does so at times. Large brown trout do no doubt take many younger trout and parr, for they need something more substantial than aquatic or terrestrial insects to sustain them. A 6 lb brown trout caught by Len Lightfoot on the Teifi in March 1972 was found to contain five sea trout smolts when it was opened up.

Eels One fish predator still shrouded in some mystery is the eel. It has never been shown with any real accuracy what an eel's diet consists of, and it is likely to vary according to whatever is available in its particular location. Eels are known to feed on invertebrates and other small fresh water animals and in so doing can be a serious competitor for food with young trout. They are also, of course, well-known fish-eaters, but how many fish they are actually able to catch alive is debatable. Years ago they were considered to be a serious predator of game fish and were often accused of digging up redds to get at the spawn. If this is the case then they are a most serious menace, for that is striking at the very heart of the production cycle. Trout eggs have been found in the stomachs of eels on limited occasions but they were probably stray eggs that would have died anyway. It is now thought likely that eels do little or no damage to sea trout or salmon redds. The major mitigating factor in their favour is that eggs incubate in the gravel during the winter months and at this time of cold water temperatures eels do not actively feed but hide away in a state of semi-hibernation in holes under stones and in the mud. They do not normally begin feeding properly (as any worm fisherman will testify) until the arrival of the warmer weather in late May or June, when all the eggs have long since hatched.

Eels will no doubt take fry and smaller fish if they can catch them, but it is doubtful that they do so in any quantity. One age-old myth that they will eat any old rubbish and scavenge extensively is completely untrue. I have caught eels for a number of years in baited traps and fyke nets, and to attract them the bait must be absolutely fresh. They show no interest in stale food.

Distribution is widespread throughout Britain and they will find their way into the most inaccessible places, for they are capable of travelling some distance over damp ground. In several sea trout rivers of the west coast, though not very big, they are present in enormous numbers. If they were seriously harmful to the fisheries then their presence would have been felt and their detrimental effect shown long before now.

On reaching the sea the number of fish-eating predators increases considerably. All members of the cod family eat fish as part of their diet, and conger eels, bass, skates, rays and sharks are pisciverous. Practically all will eat other forms of salt water life, such as molluscs and crustaceans, but the opportunity of a meal of sea trout or salmon is probably gratefully accepted when the occasion arises. The pollack lives almost entirely on a diet of fish and is very common on the south and west coasts, growing to 20 lb and more. They could possibly be the most serious fish predator on sea trout in some coastal localities. In the west of Ireland pollack have been shown to be responsible (by examination of the stomach contents) for feeding on smolts in the estuaries in the spring. Whitling are also probably eaten by larger fish.

In conclusion, it would be as well to point out the value of predation on a species in helping to maintain a balanced and healthy population. Weak or sickly individuals are weeded out (being easier for predators to catch) and so only the genes of the fittest individuals are passed on to the next generation. This is fully demonstrated by the presence of pike in a fishery; although hated by some anglers, they are, nevertheless, controlling the population and preventing large numbers of stunted unhealthy fish from developing (unless it is a fishery stocked with trout, which is in any case an artificial situation). Most sea trout rivers have sufficient spawning escapement to stock them more than adequately with fry, and so the various predators may be doing a useful job in controlling the numbers and keeping them healthy. The worst predator on sea trout, causing far more damage than any other, is man.

5

Common Diseases and Parasites

Fungus

Like all fresh water fish, sea trout are susceptible to fungus infections. The fungus, or saprolegnia as it is correctly named, can affect fish at any time of the year and at all water temperatures, though it is most commonly seen among kelts (fish which have spawned) during the autumn and winter months. It is possible that the disease is no more prevalent in cold water than in warm water, but with the larger number of fish in the river at the end of the year and the subsequent damage sustained during the rigours of spawning it spreads more easily through the population.

Its appearance is that of soggy cotton wool, very light grey in colour. A fish may be infected around an injury, the most common site for an attack, or on the fins or sometimes on the gills. In very bad cases large areas of the body may become covered and give the fish a mottled appearance. At this time they can easily be seen under the water, particularly as infected fish tend to lie in slacker water at the tail of a pool or close in towards the bank.

Many living spores are released from the fungus which can infect other fish, even to the extent of attacking healthy tissue. Sea trout kept in tanks or ponds, possibly captured and waiting to be artificially stripped of their ova, very often succumb to the disease. The first sign is several thin arcs, one or two inches in diameter, usually on the flanks or the back. In about 24 hours each one will be a completed circle and will have started to spread towards the centre. In one more day the fungus is seen as a solid white patch gradually growing larger. By the third day the infection can have spread to most parts of the body and death will follow shortly after.

There is a chemical called Malachite Green which can be flushed through the tanks or dabbed on to the infected parts to kill the fungus. It causes the fungus to slough off, and the wounds underneath are able to heal if treatment is carried out in time and reinfection is prevented. There is, of course, no practical way of treating fish in a wild situation in the river.

Saprolegnia cannot live in salt water and kelts returning to the sea after spawning quickly recover from the infection. This fungus can also be a serious problem during incubation of eggs in the gravel. Dead eggs may become infected if spores are present, and as the fungus grows the filaments quickly spread over live eggs in the redd and kill the whole batch.

Ulcerative Dermal Necrosis (UDN)

This is a serious disease affecting sea trout and salmon. Its true cause has never been discovered and a great deal of costly research has been carried out in various laboratories up and down the country. No definite conclusions have been reached and it is still not known whether it is caused by a bacterium or a virus.

A similar outbreak of disease was recorded at the turn of the last century when large numbers of salmon and sea trout are known to have died. Unfortunately, very little was understood about fish diseases at the time and few accurate records were kept as to the scale or extent of the problem. However, some old journals and papers refer to it and it seems very likely that it was the same or a similar disease to present day UDN.

The disease was first known as 'Irish salmon disease', because of the initial outbreak in southern Ireland. Later it was dubbed 'Columnaris', another disease of salmonids, but on further investigation columnaris was discounted. Ulcerative Dermal Necrosis was to be its final christening.

UDN was initially discovered in the Waterville river and Lough Currane in County Kerry, southern Ireland, in the autumn of 1964. Little notice was taken at the time because most of the infected fish were kelts and a high mortality among such fish is quite normal at this time of year. It was apparent in the spring of 1965, however, that something was wrong. Fresh-run spring fish were infected and dying, and were also turning up in other rivers in the area. By the autumn of 1965 the disease had spread to the Cork Blackwater. By early 1966 most of the southern Irish rivers contained infected fish, including the Shannon, and by 1967 the disease had spread through most of Eire and northern Ireland as well.

The first Welsh sea trout to be found with confirmed symptoms of UDN was discovered by the author in the estuary of the river Taf in June 1968.

A large sea trout with Ulcerative Dermal Necrosis (UDN) and secondary fungus infection

Table 9: Annual salmon counts at Cathleen Falls fish pass, river Erne, Ireland.

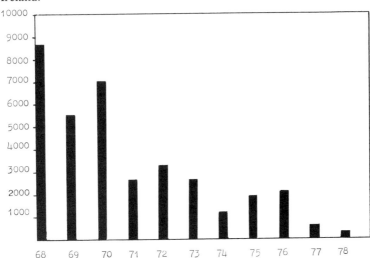

Throughout 1969 the disease continued to spread and by 1970 almost the whole of the British Isles was affected to some degree. Strangely enough, and still unexplained, several rivers scattered throughout the country did not seem to suffer too badly, and one or two appeared to escape altogether.

In Ireland, salmon was the species predominantly affected, with sea trout reportedly suffering to a much lesser extent. In Wales, however, the sea trout probably suffered a greater mortality in percentage of population than the salmon.

Disease pattern In each river the disease followed a similar pattern. In the first autumn after its appearance there was almost a total loss of fish and very little, if any, effective spawning took place. The following spring the runs of salmon and sea trout were similarly attacked, but a proportion of fish that entered later in the year spawned successfully, even though they were badly infected and died immediately after spawning. It seems unlikely that the offspring of UDN-infected parents are similarly infected. Eggs, taken in hatcheries from fish suffering from the disease, have hatched and developed normally and grown into apparently healthy fish. It could be that each generation in turn builds up some sort of immunity. The incidence in every affected river grew less over about a ten-year period and it seems probable that they are at last nearly free from the scourge that has lasted so long. We are only left with speculation as to its cause, which ranges from the dumping of nuclear waste in the sea to sunburn.

The populations of sea trout in Wales weathered the storm and have bounced back well, for they are as plentiful now as before. Not so the

salmon, however; the spring run of the larger brethren already under
intolerable pressure from high seas netting was dealt a death blow by
UDN and, despite a few game hangers-on, has virtually disappeared in
some rivers that were previously noted for spring fish.

The symptoms of UDN are easily recognised. It starts as a small, bare
skinless patch on top of the fish's head. Those parts of the body that are
not covered with scales—the head, tail and fins—seem to be most prone
to the initial attack. It is simply an 'eating away' of the flesh or, as the name
implies, 'necrosis'. In badly infected fish the bones of the top of the skull
are laid bare, and the fins and tail deteriorate until only the spines are left.
Lesions on the body can become quite deep.

In almost all cases a secondary infection of saprolegnia fungus invades
the damaged tissue, and the wounds become covered in the characteristic
white fur which is easily visible while the fish is in the water. Some disease
experts believe that because at one time there were so many fish with
fungus-attacked lesions in the rivers, the fungal spores were so widespread
that healthy fish became infected also. As a result, many fish died during
the outbreak that were not necessarily suffering from UDN.

Apart from the loss of the spring salmon run, the UDN outbreak has
left a marked difference in the number of salmon kelts, in Welsh rivers in
particular. Whereas in the pre-outbreak days kelts were present in numbers, sometimes even till late May, very few are caught these days even at
the start of the season. Perhaps after spawning they migrate back quickly
to the healthier salt water before any fungal infections set in or to clear
away those that have begun.

In Ireland, too, UDN has left its mark. At a fish pass counter at Kath-
leen Falls on the river Erne the number of salmon dropped from just under
9,000 in 1968 to 297 in 1978. Fisheries workers attributed the major
proportion of the decline to UDN.

Furunculosis

This disease is very common among sea trout and, given the right conditions to manifest itself, can cause heavy mortalities in low-water conditions during the summer. It is caused by a bacterium that lives in the
blood and is always present in both wild and hatchery-reared fish. When
fish become stressed, as when the water temperatures are high and dissolved oxygen levels are low, the bacteria may rapidly cause infection as they
multiply in the blood.

The disease very often proves fatal and some fish may die without any
external sign of the cause, but more commonly boils or furuncules (from
whence the disease gets its name) are formed on the sides of the fish and
can be easily seen as raised swellings, usually filled with blood. The
furuncules often burst, resulting in rapid death and the release of millions
of bacteria into the water which will infect other fish.

The disease rarely appears until the water temperatures reach 10°C, and
the warmer the water the more likely an outbreak is to occur. Where there

are concentrations of sea trout in lower pools of the river and the river is down to summer level with high temperatures, such as happened in the summers of 1976 and 1983, large numbers of fish may die.

In north-eastern America and Canada the disease is a problem during the hot summers experienced in that area. Many salmon in such famous rivers as the Restigouche and the Miramichi are lost in some years due to furunculosis.

The disease was once dreaded in fish farms and hatcheries. There was no known cure, and as soon as it was suspected in a pond the fish were destroyed and buried as quickly as possible and the pond drained and disinfected. There is a much better understanding of diseases in today's modern units and antibiotic drugs like 'Tribrissen' and 'Chloramphenicol' have greatly reduced the devastating losses experienced at one time. Provided the symptoms are recognised and the disease diagnosed at an early stage these treatments can be administered at the correct dosages, mixed with the food, and losses of fish are minimal. Fish can also be treated by injection, for instance valuable brood stock, but there is unfortunately no practical method of treating fish in a wild situation.

Sea Lice

Sea lice (scientific name, *lepeoptherius*) are very common on fresh-run sea trout and salmon throughout the British Isles. Their presence on a fish caught in the river confirms that it has recently entered from the sea and is in prime condition, and sometimes they will even increase its commercial value. The sea louse, a salt water parasite, is a small invertebrate animal up to one quarter of an inch long (6 mm). Oval in shape, the females sometimes have long egg sacs attached to them but these are rarely seen unless the fish is really fresh, for they quickly drop off in fresh water. The commonest site of infection is on top and around the head, on the back and in the adipose fin region of the tail, but they may be found on any part of the fish's body. They feed by rasping on the skin with their powerful jaws and devouring the resulting bits of tissues. Damaged areas may become infected with other disease organisms, particularly fungus. At one time there was a theory that UDN and sea-lice lesions were possibly connected and this has still not been entirely ruled out. Is it a mere coincidence that the sea louse's favourite site is also the area for most common UDN attack —the top of the head?

Sometimes even quite small whitling, fresh from the tide, are covered with dozens of these creatures; the jumping and flashing of fish in pools near the sea is probably due to the skin irritation caused, making the fish rub and shake in an endeavour to get rid of the lice.

This parasite cannot live in fresh water for very long and most will drop off after about twenty-four hours. Opinions vary as to the actual length of time they may remain attached to the fish and it is known that they live longer in cold water, but it is unlikely that they would survive more than about three days.

In some years they can cause considerable damage to salmon being reared artificially in sea cages. There is, however, little scope for any treatment, since our coastal waters contain millions of the juvenile stages of this creature waiting to attach themselves to any host that happens along.

Gill Maggots

Gill maggots (scientific name, *salmincola*) are common parasites of salmon and large sea trout. Small sea trout and whitling are very rarely affected, possibly because of the large size of these organisms. Slightly smaller than sea lice and longer in appearance, they can be seen attached to the ends of the gill filaments and are very often present in fish that have been in fresh water for a long time. Though a fresh water parasite they can withstand salt water for fairly long periods, and a fish that goes back to the sea as a kelt may still have some of them attached on its return to the river. The presence of gill maggots on a fresh-run fish is a sure sign that it is a previous spawner and on a return spawning journey. The gill maggots do not cause serious damage to the fish unless they are present in large numbers, when the protective mucus discharge on the gills and the damage to the gill filaments can badly affect the fish's ability to obtain sufficient oxygen. Sometimes the injuries to the gill filaments can leave the affected areas open to invasion by other disease organisms, especially fungus.

Possibly the worst aspect of the parasite is its offensive appearance, and many anglers and commercial fishermen clean off the gills when an infected fish is caught.

Lampreys

Although it can be argued that lampreys are predators, they are nevertheless, strictly speaking, parasites. They are very similar in shape and size to eels and are often mistaken for them, but on closer examination they are quite different.

A lamprey's mouth is at the front of the head on the underside and consists of a circular sucker with rows of sharp teeth. It feeds by fastening itself on to the side of a fish by its sucker, rasping the flesh away with its teeth and eating the loosened tissues. This is in a similar fashion to the sea louse, but because the lamprey is much larger the resulting wound is bigger and deeper.

The sucker is also used to hold on to stones and obstructions in fast currents when trying to ascend a river; even so they are not strong swimmers and are unable to surmount even modest obstructions. It is possible that at times they are able to move over moist ground in a similar fashion to eels, but as far as I know there are no records of this happening. Their limited mobility restricts them to the lower and middle reaches of the larger rivers that are without any substantial rapids or other obstructions. They must have sufficient gravel to spawn and there must also be mud banks for the larvae (called *ammocoete*) to inhabit and develop away from predators. The Towy and the Taf are two such suitable rivers and both have sizeable runs of sea lampreys in the early summer.

Brook Lamprey The brook lamprey, which is the smallest, spends its whole life in fresh water. It lives in muddy banks of clear, fast trout streams, and where it does occur is quite plentiful though rarely seen, owing to its habits of concealment. It only emerges from its muddy home to feed on invertebrate insects and plankton. This species, light brown in colour and growing to about a maximum of six inches, is not parasitic on fish.

River Lamprey Another type, the river lamprey, is slightly larger and has a similar migratory life style to the sea trout. After hatching it spends up to four years in the river and then descends to the sea. The adults return to the river in shoals in May or early June, usually during a flood. They are then silver in colour and average about 12 inches (30 centimetres) in length.

In some years river lampreys enter the rivers in vast shoals, thousands strong, and in others there will be few or even none at all. They ascend rivers as high as obstructions will allow, and spawn over shallow, fast-flowing gravel beds during June and July. The redds are very similar in appearance to small trout redds; the lampreys move the pebbles by sucking on to them and positioning them as required. After spawning all the adults die.

In the last century these fish were known as 'lamperns' and commercial fisheries existed on some rivers, especially the larger ones like the Severn, Thames and Trent, where they were caught in special traps, called 'wheels' or 'leaps'.

The awesome sucker mouth of a sea lamprey

There is little evidence that river lampreys cause damage to sea trout stocks, even though they are parasitic on fish in the sea (they do not feed in the river). As they enter the river before the main run of sea trout arrives it is possible that any fish that have been attacked have died or their wounds healed, and this particular lamprey's handiwork is never seen.

Sea Lamprey The third, and by far the largest, of these parasitic fish is the sea lamprey. Like the river lamprey it migrates to the sea at three or four years of age, and on return it is unmistakenly identified by its size. The adults are up to 25 inches long (65 centimetres) and are a dirty, mottled brown. They enter fresh water from mid-May to the end of July, and spawn on gravel beds in the lower reaches.

A pair will make a redd as large as, and similar to, a salmon's or large sea trout's, carefully moving the stones with their sucker mouths. The appearance of these redds has in the past resulted in reports of salmon and sea trout spawning out of season, the redds being mistakenly identified.

After spawning the adult fish all die and the hatched larvae drop down to live in the estuary mud until they have grown large enough to migrate to the sea. Many years ago sea lampreys were eaten as a delicacy but the only demand now for such an unappetising looking fish is for university research.

The amount of damage done to salmon and sea trout by sea lampreys is unknown, but it may be considerable. Salmon and larger sea trout are caught from time to time with lamprey marks on them, usually in the form of a circular sore about one and a half inches in diameter. The point of attack is usually in the region below the lateral line on the belly.

In North America some years ago the invasion of sea lampreys in the Great Lakes resulted in an almost complete extinguishing of the population of lake trout and upset the whole species balance in those fisheries.

6

Management of the Resource

The Effects of Man's Activities

If man had not over-populated, industrialised and polluted the environment, there is no doubt that sea trout would be present in more rivers, have a much wider range and be far more numerous than they are today. Throughout the last two hundred years, and particularly from the time of the industrial revolution, man's search for knowledge and technical advancement and his growth towards modern civilisation have often been carried out at the expense of the environment, and especially of animal life. Fish are no exception and have sometimes been thoughtlessly dismissed as a needless and expendable commodity that can be sacrificed for the sake of progress. It is only now, at this late stage, that natural resources have begun to receive the attention they deserve. At last it is being realised that a healthy environment for all living things cannot but be of benefit to man himself.

A lesson has been learned: the past damage caused to rivers by pollution, the building of dams, over-fishing, abstraction, drainage and other abuses has come to a halt but is still very evident in fishless streams and a ravaged aquatic environment. Laws have been passed and moral obligations fully realised so that the process will, in time, be reversed. How long it will take is anyone's guess. The havoc wreaked during the last hundred years will probably take just as long to put right and even though the uphill struggle has started there is still a mountain to climb. Past great fishing rivers, like the Thames, Trent, Tees and Tyne, have begun to see a major improvement in their water quality, and stretches that were fishless twenty years ago are now showing signs of a slow recovery. Today's legislation prevents new industry from developing on the basis that a watercourse is the ideal site for the dumping of waste materials. Sadly, many people still consider that a river is the easiest and most convenient place in which to dispose of rubbish.

Fortunately, the main sea trout strongholds of Wales, Ireland and Scotland escaped such ravages, owing to their outlying inaccessibility. However, some areas suffered through mining activities, and industry, particularly in south Wales, took its toll. The Rheidol was fishless thirty years ago, due to lead and zinc poisoning from the Cardiganshire mines. Fish in the Taff, Ebbw and Sirhowy, among others, suffered death from

71

industrial wastes. The Rheidol has recovered and is now a fine sea trout river, and some of the south Wales rivers are gaining ground year by year. Even so, the most serious threat to sea trout populations is still pollution, which can be caused in various ways, not least by deliberate poacher poisoning. This is an act which deserves no clemency to the perpetrators, for it kills all fish and does not select the larger individuals.

Pollution Pollution can be either organic or inorganic. Organic pollution is caused by natural waste products, such as sewage, farm effluent or trade effluent from food processing. The result of organic pollution is a drop in dissolved oxygen levels, possibly to a level below that at which fish can live. Vast amounts of minute organisms feed on the waste material in the water and use up oxygen to such an extent that serious oxygen depletion can occur. A few poisonous agricultural chemicals also come into the organic category.

Inorganic pollution is usually associated with industry, and includes a variety of acids and poisons. Though many are toxic to fish, such as salts of heavy metals like lead, copper and zinc, some cause death due to a sudden change in pH or because the pH is moved outside the range at which fish can live. Inorganic pollutants are a continuing menace in areas of heavy industry and active mining, and although legislation has curbed their damaging influence to a certain extent accidents still occur far too frequently, when toxic substances are allowed to enter a river. The smallest watercourse or ditch will eventually empty into a river and the discharge need not be directly into a stream to cause harm.

Pollution control is the responsibility of the regional Water Authorities in England and Wales, and their officers keep a close watch and carry out monitoring programmes on known sources of pollution. It is the duty of any angler, or any other citizen for that matter, to report suspected pollution to the nearest offices of the local Water Authority. There is a 24-hour call-out service and complaints are normally dealt with at once.

Land drainage There is an ever-growing lobby of both anglers and conservationists against the actions of Water Authorities' land drainage engineers. These days proposed schemes are examined in detail before any work is carried out and all interested parties such as fisheries, recreation and nature conservation organisations, are consulted to minimise any damage which a particular scheme may cause. It is a sad fact that this was not always the case in the past. Some drainage schemes, carried out by the old River Authorities in particular, went ahead with little consideration for the likely impact on the environment and, especially fisheries.

Many sea trout rivers in Wales, following a series of drainage schemes on them, have become fast, efficient drainage channels to carry away heavy mountain rainfall as quickly as possible without flooding adjacent land. There is no doubt that the work done has greatly benefitted agriculture and stock farming. Large areas of boggy, swampy land are now fit for grazing and growing crops, whereas before they were only suitable as habitats for the likes of frogs and nesting curlews.

Some changes are far-reaching, however, and the river Aeron in west Wales is a prime example of the way continuous drainage schemes have completely altered a river's profile and behaviour. The middle reaches of the Aeron valley contained many hundreds of acres of unusable marshy land. This acted as a gigantic sponge and during the summer in dry weather the river was continuously supplied from the many springs which kept the river level up. The river has now been turned into a drainage channel, the bed deepened, bends removed and pools destroyed. Heavy rain results in extremely fast run-off to the sea. This means that the river rises very rapidly and equally quickly runs off again—a flood is gone in a day (heavy water used to last for two or three days and only ran off slowly).

All these drainage works have had two major effects on the sea trout's environment, one good and one bad. With the straightening of the course and the quickening of the flow the amount of spawning gravel has increased tremendously and these large areas of shallow, gravelly runs are ideal habitat for fry and parr, unlike the slow, deep, muddy stretches that existed before. Land drainage works have, therefore, in all probability, increased production in some cases. The returning adult fish, however, no longer have the necessary deep pools in which to rest up and hide. With the disappearance of the holding pools the sea trout have little protection from predators and poachers. Even on stretches where drainage operations have not been carried out, the gravel loosened by the drag lines upstream has caused many of the deep holding pools in the lower reaches to fill in. In some cases river temperatures get higher in shallow water during the summer, which results in low oxygen levels, stressed fish, disease and death. So, even though the production of juveniles may have increased, the angling value of waters, normally judged by the amount and quality of the holding pools present, has significantly decreased.

The trend for salmon runs to become later and later each year and the decrease in spring-run fish is generally blamed on UDN and netting at sea, but a contributing factor may be the amount of dredging that has been carried out on some rivers. It is no longer safe for the fish to enter the rivers till the autumn rains arrive and provide reasonable flows. Sea trout, being smaller, are able to find refuge in lower water conditions, but it is possible that they, too, will eventually learn that a later ascent of the river will be safer and, therefore, more productive.

Fishery owners who have not been consulted or consider that damage has been done by land drainage engineers, with lost fishing as a result, should seek recompense. Very often this may entail some sort of improvement to the water, such as groynes or weirs, constructed at the Authority's expense. Water Authority Fisheries' officers will be only too glad to advise on fisheries' interests if called upon to do so. The important thing is to become involved before any plans or estimates of works have been drawn up, for it may be too late once work has started.

Agriculture Modern agricultural practices have affected rivers in some areas. To produce more and better crops from the land the use of fertilising chemicals is now widespread. The result of this is that the land becomes richer in nutrients, and these nitrates and phosphates will eventually find their way into watercourses and rivers and enrich the aquatic environment to such an extent that the species present may change. An abundance of weed where there was little before is a sure sign that the water is becoming more eutrophic (the biologists' term for a rich and highly productive water). Weed beds may cause silting and a resulting loss of spawning gravel for salmonids. Heavy plant growth can also result in serious depletion of dissolved oxygen at night.

Abstraction Water may be abstracted from a river (with Water Authority approval) for a variety of reasons. Some industries use it merely for cooling purposes after which it is returned in almost the same condition and quality as when it was removed, albeit sometimes at a higher temperature. Other processes like brewing or canning actually use a large amount of the water which is not returned. Some factories use the water and then return it, but it is used in such a way that it has to be treated extensively before being returned.

Abstraction for crop irrigation is a total loss of water to the river, as all of it is taken up by plant growth or lost through evaporation. Water abstraction for potable use is carried out in many areas and most larger rivers lose some of their water in this way. It is not totally lost to the river, however, in that a great deal is returned by way of treated sewage effluent, but usually much further downstream than the abstraction point.

The Water Authorities control abstraction by issuing licences and the procedure for doing so is such that any parties likely to be injured, for example, an angling club or private fishery owner, can object before a

Llyn Brianne Dam at the top of the Towy

A smolt trap upstream of Llyn Brianne

licence is granted. This may or may not result in a refusal to grant the licence, depending on the likely destructive effect of the proposed abstraction.

Dam Building The building of dams to provide hydro electric power or for reservoir impoundment can have a most serious effect on a sea trout river. Firstly, the upper reaches become inaccessible and large amounts of spawning areas and juvenile habitat may be lost. Secondly, the natural rhythm of floods and fluctuating river levels, common to such streams, may be altered and fish may prefer to enter neighbouring rivers with a more normal flow.

In North America in the last hundred years or so the widespread practice of building dams for hydro power has resulted in almost every river of any size having at least one insurmountable obstruction on it and, in some cases, several. This has caused substantial losses of migratory fish runs throughout the country and only now has the problem begun to be tackled by the construction of fish passes and restocking from hatcheries.

Fortunately, the development of hydro power in the British Isles has not been so prominent, with the possible exception of Scotland. The building of dams for reservoirs has also been limited to a certain extent, for in Britain there are numerous natural lakes which have gone a long way towards satisfying the insatiable need for water. Nevertheless, many reservoirs have had to be, and still are being, built.

To safeguard the salmon and sea trout at such sites many schemes have been devised to protect the species as far as possible. Rivers are restocked from hatcheries to compensate for the loss of spawning grounds above the dams. Also, trapping and trucking around the obstructions to allow the fish to carry on upstream are carried out in some cases. Despite large sums of money being spent in several areas, no method has yet been found, and is unlikely to be, to compensate fully for the loss of natural habitat.

Legislation

Salmon and Freshwater Fisheries Act An essential safeguard to control the important sea trout resource is legislation. An Act of Parliament, the Salmon and Freshwater Fisheries Act of 1975, lays down certain laws to control illegal fishing, times of close seasons and various other necessary regulations. Part 1 of the Act deals entirely with the prohibition of certain methods of taking fish, which includes instruments such as jigs (Aberaeron minnows), set lines and even firearms. It prohibits the use of any fish roe as bait, covers the deliberate discharge of poisons or other toxic substances into the river and also makes illegal the use of explosives or electric devices.

Part 2 governs the obstruction to the passage of fish and makes it illegal to prevent migratory fish from ascending a river by building obstructions without an approved fish pass or failing to maintain one that is already in existence.

Part 3 deals with the times of fishing and close seasons, and Part 4 with the power of the Water Authorities to issue fishing licences.

Duties of the Water Authorities Part 5 of the Salmon and Freshwater Fisheries Act makes it the duty of the Water Authorities to maintain, improve and develop the salmon fisheries, trout fisheries, fresh water fisheries and eel fisheries in their areas. The 1975 Act was the first Fisheries Act to provide statutory requirements for the Water Authorities actually to look after the fisheries resource in this way, and a large part of an Authority's fisheries functions is now to give professional advice to those who require it.

In England and Wales the regional Water Authorities were set up by the Water Act of 1973. Previously there were many more, smaller river authorities, water supply boards and sewage boards which were all amalgamated into the new, much larger authorities.

The old river authorities and the water boards before them did little to promote the growth of fisheries, apart from acting as guardians, issuing licences, making byelaws to protect the existing resource and providing a bailiff force to enforce the fisheries laws. Under the new Act the Water Authorities were also instructed to establish fisheries advisory committees, consisting of members who had an interest in fisheries in their region, and to consult such committees as to the manner in which fisheries improvement and development should take place.

Bye Laws Although the Salmon and Fresh Water Fisheries Act provides a wide ranging spectrum of fisheries legislation, each Water Authority is empowered to make bye laws covering its area to suit local conditions. Any bye laws must, however, be confirmed by the Minister of Agriculture, Fisheries and Food before they actually become law.

Bye laws may be made for a variety of reasons with the express purpose of fisheries conservation. The most important ones are those which govern local variations in the fishing seasons. Guidelines are set down by the Act, which, for instance, states that the salmon close season shall have a minimum duration of one hundred and fifty three days. Other bye laws will deal with the use of lures and baits, possibly banning some in certain areas, restricting the size of hooks allowed, and so on. There are also bye laws governing the methods used by commercial fishermen, the areas and times they may fish, and the length and mesh size of nets. Every angler should make himself familiar with the bye laws operating in his own particular area.

When a Water Authority wishes to make a new bye law it must advertise the fact so that any objections can be made by persons who may have a valid reason for disagreeing with it. If objections are strong, then the Minister may require that a public enquiry be held to discuss the issue to enable him to reach a decision on whether to approve it or not. This elaborate procedure for making bye laws is to prevent them being made in haste without proper consultation with interested parties and due consideration being given to their true value or effects. If a bye law is made that has a detrimental effect on a fishery, a claim for damages may be made against the Authority.

One important fact that is sometimes overlooked is that bye laws, once made, become the law of the land, carrying summary penalities, and are not just petty rules to be disregarded.

Fisheries' Improvement

Artificial propagation It was known many years ago that trout and salmon could be artificially spawned and reared in hatcheries and ponds, and at the end of the last century there were several fish farms in the United Kingdom rearing fish for restocking rivers and lakes. There has been a tremendous upsurge in the trout farming industry since the war and particularly so since about 1970. There are now many farms rearing trout for both the table and for restocking purposes (mainly trout fisheries in reservoirs). In Scotland and Ireland salmon rearing in cages in salt water has become an important industry as it has on some parts of the continent, mainly Norway. The present production from Norwegian salmon farms exceeds 15,000 tonnes annually.

Like all the other salmonids, sea trout can be stripped (the term used for the actual taking of the eggs) and their eggs hatched and reared on to the smolt stage, when they can be released to begin their journey to the sea.

To release smolts from hatcheries is not, however, the ultimate solution in ensuring future stocks of sea trout, for there are several disadvantages in this form of stock enhancement. Rearing fish is a very costly business. The capital costs of setting up a fish farm are high, because of the price of land and the subsequent buildings, including roads, tanks, ponds and pipework, all of which have to be constructed. Rearing costs are also high, because of labour charges and the expensive specially-prepared fish food pellets. Fish farming is very much a risk business and at any time fish may be lost through bad management, floods or disease.

There is serious doubt as to whether hatchery-reared smolts are as viable as wild ones. They do not receive a natural diet, are not wise to the dangers of predation and are not at all as strong and fit as fish which have grown naturally in the river and have had to fend for themselves. Very often the hatchery smolts will be released a long way from the rearing site or even on a different river system altogether, and they may become disorientated to such an extent that their homing instinct will be seriously impaired when they wish to return from the sea.

Despite all these drawbacks there are still occasions when smolts could be a useful way of replenishing a fishery. For instance, a river that has long suffered from pollution would probably benefit from smolt release initially to get some spawners back as quickly as possible to begin the cycle of reproduction. They would also be an excellent way of replenishing stocks after serious accidental pollution.

Restocking can take place at any stage in the cycle, with eggs planted in artificial redds, ready-to-feed fry, and fed fry or parr all being stages which can be considered and each one judged on its merits. Generally speaking, the earlier stage that is stocked the less expense, but the higher mortality. A stretch of river above an obstruction would be an ideal place to stock with fry to utilise the unused areas that adult sea trout cannot reach. Any tributary or area of a river where spawning gravel is scarce or non-existent would be a good site for the planting of eyed eggs so that they would hatch naturally and make use of the vacant habitat.

Other factors must be taken into consideration before rushing into a restocking policy, however, for it may turn out to be an expensive waste that could have been avoided. Can an obstruction be removed or destroyed or a fish pass installed, or can improvements be made to the stream habitat? Artificial propagation has an established place in the management of fisheries, but other perhaps equally important methods of stock enhancement should be considered, maybe in conjunction with it.

Removal of unwanted species Removal of unwanted species in a sea trout river would usually mean the removal of the brown trout which prey on the young fry and parr and also compete with them for the available food. The difficulty here is that there is no way of telling which fish of less than about six inches are sea trout and which are brown trout. Probably the only safe way would be to remove all trout over six inches, since these would most likely be browns as any sea trout of that size would have migrated downstream towards the sea or else have smolted and so be easily identified. Removal of brown trout above an obstruction before stocking with sea trout eggs or fry can be done totally, for if the stream is inaccessible to upstream migrants then all the trout present will be browns.

Some years ago the practice of clearing streams of brown trout (or young sea trout) before stocking with salmon fry was commonplace. This was usually done by Water Authority staff by electric fishing and was very time-consuming. The method is not favoured so much nowadays for several reasons that have become apparent. The removal of all fish is impossible and any remaining brown trout, together with recruits from further upstream and from tributaries, soon repopulate the stretch. There is even evidence to suggest that the recolonisation by brown trout produces a stronger and fitter population than before, therefore making such an exercise detrimental and not beneficial as was the intention.

The only way to clear a stream effectively of all trout is to use 'rotenone', or a similar chemical poison that can be used under controlled conditions to kill the fish present. The little damage that is caused to invertebrates quickly repairs itself by repopulation and then stocking can prove most beneficial in terms of recruit numbers to that river system. Though condemned by some as far too drastic a measure, the benefits in increased productivity of a required species can make a significant difference and it is surprising that this method does not find wider favour.

Brown trout anglers would be shocked at such a suggestion, but the fact is that very many small sea trout rivers have such small and stunted brown trout populations, because of fast flows and lack of food, that they are of no use whatsoever to anglers. The use of poisons is strictly controlled by legislation and permission must be obtained from the local Water Authority, which in turn must obtain the approval of the Minister.

There are many cases on record of improved fisheries performance when an unwanted competitor species is removed or thinned out. The trapping and removal of perch from Loughs Corrib and Mask in Ireland saw, over a number of years, a considerable increase in the numbers and weight of brown trout caught. The removal of pike from reservoir trout fisheries has long been common practice. The presence of pike in a sea trout river would be highly undesirable and they should be removed whenever possible, particularly if there are no prey fish like gudgeon, roach or bream to divert their attentions from the parr and smolts.

Stream improvement Stream improvements may be undertaken for two reasons, one to improve the fishes' habitat and the other to improve the angling. Those carried out to improve the stream habitat and, therefore, its production of fish are generally beyond the scope of individual fishery owners and are normally done by the Water Authorities. These can include desilting, deweeding or even introducing new gravel to increase spawning. It is unlikely that a fishery owner would want to carry out such exercises at his own expense, since the benefit would be to the whole of the river and not to one particular stretch.

There are several ways to improve a length of water to make it more 'fishable' and produce more fish for anglers who use it. Cases for treatment as a rule are shallow, fast-water areas where the land drainage engineer's work has taken effect. Sometimes fisheries' improvements will have been undertaken as part of a drainage scheme, but if not there are some fairly simple methods of creating holding water in such areas. The most practical is to build bankside groynes, which has the effect of concentrating the current flow to scour out the river bed and create areas of deeper water. A popular method, though quite costly and labour-intensive, is to build

Gabion groynes will form pools in fast, shallow stretches

gabion buttresses. These are a kind of strong wire mesh cage which are constructed on the site and then filled with stones. Such structures are used extensively by Water Authorities' engineers to strengthen and stabilise river banks and prevent erosion near to installations such as buildings, roads or railway lines. As a rule, two are needed on opposite sides to work efficiently and create a pool. They are so designed that during heavy flows the flood water rises over the top of them while still contained within the river's banks. Another effect, and one of the reasons why these structures are favoured by river engineers, is that as water scour creates more depth the gabions tend to sink in the river bed as well and, therefore, alleviate the flooding problems which might arise with a fixed, more permanent structure. If only one is used then there may be erosion caused to the opposite bank, which will cause problems, especially if it belongs to someone else. In all cases where work on the river bed is intended or any structure is to be placed in it, permission must first be sought from the Water Authority.

Two simple current deflectors which will create scouring and form fish-holding pools are the post-and-batten type and the stone groyne. Neither will last for a lengthy period unless carefully maintained, as winter floods in particular tend to be most unkind to such structures. A stretch of water can be greatly improved for anglers by the careful and selective

The materials required for gabion construction

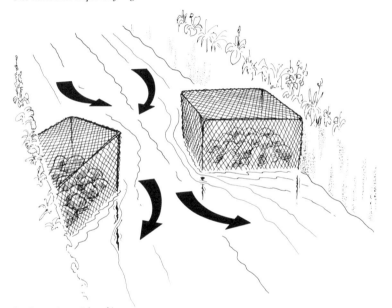

Pool creation with gabion groynes

cutting of trees and bushes. However, cutting down trees and branches obscuring a pool to make easier casting room needs to be done with some care and thought, for overhanging bushes are favourite lies for sea trout. They particularly like the shade of an overhanging willow or alder.

There are also several ways that life can be made more comfortable for the angler on a stretch of water. Proper stiles over hedges or barbed wire fences are a boon, as are adequate car parking and the provision of paths and the proper placement of signs to direct and mark fishing boundaries. Many beats are divided along the banks by feeder streams or deep ditches, and a simple log bridge can be built to make access that much easier.

A roughly made wooden hut can be a splendid addition for shelter from the rain or a sit-down retreat for flask and sandwiches, or even a yarn with fellow anglers.

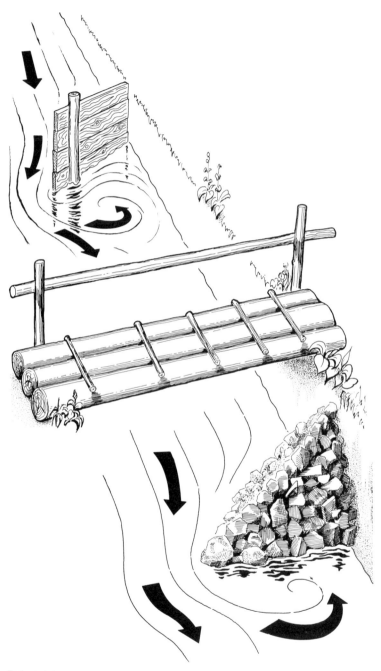

Fisheries' improvements

Rheidol Falls. The entrance to the fish pass is on the right.

*A pool and weir fish pass blasted out of solid rock on the river
Liscomb, Nova Scotia*

*A pool and weir fish pass made out of timber on the Mersey
river, Nova Scotia*

Fish passes The provision of fish passes to allow migratory salmonids to travel upstream to spawning grounds past obstructions they would otherwise be unable to surmount is an important conservation measure. They may be employed at natural obstructions, thereby opening up new waters, or, as more often is the case, at man-made obstructions to allow fish to proceed where they previously did, without hindrance.

Natural obstructions are best removed altogether, possibly by explosives, but the next best method is to provide a fish pass. There are still many miles of river unavailable to sea trout and salmon because of natural barriers to their migration, and there is no doubt that their removal could contribute the greatest stock increase potential of all conservation measures.

A denil fish pass at Ennistimon, Co. Clare, Ireland

In this modern age of conservation awareness it is unlikely, if not impossible, for any man-made structure to be built without some form of fish passage or other related scheme, such as trapping and trucking or compensation re-stocking on an annual basis. The Salmon and Freshwater Fisheries Act makes it an obligation to provide fish passage facilities at any new obstruction if the river in question is frequented by salmon or sea trout. This was not so in the past, however, and large rivers like the

Thames and Trent had mill weirs, navigation weirs, dams and sluices built on them with little regard to the necessary upstream migration of salmonids to their spawning grounds. The result was that some of the largest runs of salmon that Britain has ever seen, or is ever likely to, died out completely. There are several types of fish passes, each one suited to different locations, depending on height, width and flow velocities. The simplest form of pass is a box constructed at the base of a vertical weir, effectively dividing the obstruction into two easy stages. One jump into the box and, following a short rest, another jump to surmount the weir. A vertical waterfall of about six feet high can quite easily be fitted with a box pass.

A pool and weir pass, which is a very old design, can be made to enable fish to scale considerable heights. As a rule, the higher the obstruction the bigger the pass needs to be in terms of volume. If the pass is a long one then larger resting pools, constructed at intervals, will be required.

A denil pass is another popular form, particularly in Ireland, and is known to work very well. A denil pass constructed at Ennistimon in County Clare enables salmon and sea trout to surmount a natural obstacle some sixty feet high, and has created a run of migratory fish where none existed before. The baffle boards of a denil are so designed that the velocity of water remains constant throughout the length of the pass. Again, resting pools are sometimes provided at intervals if the pass is a long one. All passes are prone to blockage by debris, especially during floods, and a denil is no exception and needs to be maintained regularly.

If the obstruction is extremely large, like a reservoir dam, then a Borland fish lock may be used. This device is so constructed that fish are attracted into a chamber by a flow of water, and at intervals, usually on a time clock, a sluice closes and traps them in. The chamber then fills up from above and the fish swim up a flume into the reservoir or river upstream.

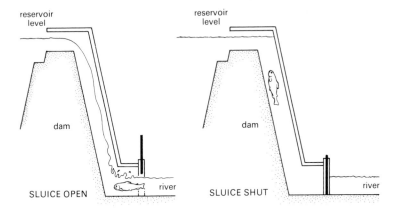

A borland Fish pass

7
Fly Fishing

Flies

These days it must be difficult for beginners to fly fishing to decide on what fly or flies to choose from several hundreds of patterns. Judging by the assortment that some anglers carry with them while fishing, as though they are determined not to be caught short without a particular pattern, it might appear that such a collection is necessary, but this is far from the case.

It is often said that fish cannot tell the difference between patterns. I feel certain that no fish can tell if a fly has a wing of partridge feather or pheasant tail, or a body of hare's fur or wool, but they *can* distinguish shape and size and most certainly some of the brighter shades and colours. Colour is probably the least important feature of the fly, however, because a fish's view of the fly is, for much of the time, against the sky and therefore it can only be seen as a dark outline. This is very much the case when fishing at night.

For sea trout fishing only a handful of patterns are necessary, though a selection of sizes in each chosen dressing is a must. My choice of twelve patterns, six for the day and six for the night, in different sizes will serve to cover all eventualities. Sea trout flies are generally brightly dressed compared with normal trout flies, but are not as elaborate as those for salmon, which in their fully dressed form are better displayed as works of artistic beauty (and often are) than used to catch fish. Trout flies are, on the other hand, usually dressed to imitate a natural insect to fool the fish into thinking that it is seizing a natural meal. Many sea trout flies, like those for salmon, do not imitate a living creature but possibly resemble a small fish and, therefore, awaken the fish's predatory instinct, or else remind it of some sea creature eaten with relish in its not-too-distant past.

I would never fish for sea trout with a fly that did not have gold or silver (preferably silver) incorporated in the body. Even then, total confidence is only present if the fly has a *completely* silver body. This is purely my own personal preference, probably because in the past such a fly has rewarded me with my best catches. Other anglers will prefer a bit of red, a blue hackle, a yellow tail, and so on and so forth, according to their own fads and fancies. It could be argued that a certain fly which is used almost all the time is bound to be the one that produces the most fish. The flash of a silver body no doubt has a special attraction by day and at dusk. After sunset it still seems to be the best fly, though it is hard to believe that the fish can distinguish this feature in the darkness.

Confidence, as already mentioned, plays a big part in any form of angling, as it does in most sports: the tennis player must have confidence in his racket, the snooker player in his cue, etc. The angler must have confidence in his tackle and particularly in what he is using as bait to lure the fish.

The importance of shape cannot be over-emphasised, as this is what a fish sees primarily in a lure and, coupled with its movement through the water, makes up the attractiveness of the fly. It should be streamlined and, when moving in the water, should bear a close resemblance to the shape of the fish itself. The head should be small and pointed, with a slight body bulge tapering to a point towards the tail. This refers to the shape of the fly in the water discounting the hook. There should not be a large head or a bulky tail section, both of which will transform the fly into an uninviting, awkward shape. It should be tied evenly so that it swims on an even keel and does not twist in the current as it is drawn in. This particular fault is common in winged flies, and is caused by the wings being of unequal size and not being carefully tied in straight and evenly.

Sea trout flies—multi-hooked patterns and a fully dressed Night Hawk (centre)

The whole should have a slim 'ear-of-corn' appearance in the water. Bushy flies that have a bulky outline are of little use during the day and none at all during the night. Many shop-bought flies are much too heavily dressed and it is a good idea to trim them somewhat before use. The shape referred to, of course, is in the water, when the fly is wet, and is not its appearance when dry, the two being quite different.

I will not explain the reasons for my choice of flies apart from the major one, which is that these patterns have, over the years, proved most successful for me.

For the day

March Brown: Though designed as a brown trout fly and an imitation of a natural insect, it is nevertheless very good and much used for sea trout fishing during the day. It is a drab fly, unlike the traditional sea trout patterns. It possibly resembles (to the fish) a drowned dung fly and may bring recollection of avid feeding in the river as a parr in the recent past. Best sizes are 8 down to 12. Use on a bright day when dung flies are about, this being the opposite of the age-old salmon fishing axiom of dull days requiring a dull fly, and vice versa.
Body: Hare's fur
Wings: Hen pheasant wing
Hackle: Partridge back
Tail: Two strands as hackle

Connemara Black: A favourite pattern in Ireland, from whence it gets its name. A bright fly effective in fast runs and rougher water. This fly is particularly good in slightly coloured water fining off after a spate (especially useful for the purist who does not wish to spin). Best used in larger sizes 4 and 6.
Body: Black wool ribbed oval silver tinsel
Wings: Bronze mallard
Hackle: Black and blue mixed (blue jay)
Tail: Golden pheasant crest

Mallard and Claret: This ever popular fly was the favourite of the late Ted Holder, for many years chairman of the Aberaeron town angling club and whose expertise in fly fishing had to be seen to be believed. He used it to great effect on the Aeron and Teifi in a size 10 or 12.
Body: Claret wool ribbed gold wire
Wings: Bronze mallard
Hackle: Light red
Tail: Golden pheasant tippet

Teal and Red: One of the teal wing series that so well imitates small fish fry with the scale effect of the barred wings. Can be used in large sizes in heavy water.
Body: Red wool ribbed gold tinsel
Wings: Teal flank

Hackle: Red
Tail: Golden pheasant tippet

Teal and Black: A different coloured variation of the red and used in the same fashion. If one does not work, then the other should.
Body: Black wool ribbed flat silver tinsel
Wings: Teal flank
Hackle: Black
Tail: Golden pheasant tippet

Grouse and Claret Silver Tip: A good whitling fly in low water on a bright day. Use in shallow fast water in small sizes, 10 down to 14.
Body: Tail half silver tinsel, fore half red wool
Wings: Grouse tail
Hackle: Red
Tail: Golden pheasant tippet

For the night

Butcher: A good fly in the day but even better at night, the butcher is said to be taken as a small fish and for this reason I know fly fishermen who will not use it, saying that it is not true fly fishing. This is a strange attitude indeed and I suspect that the name has something to do with it. Could it be that the person who uses it is fearful of being thought of in a similar vein? Love it or hate it, it is a sea trout killer and sometimes proves irresistible when all other patterns fail.
Body: Flat silver tinsel
Wings: Blue sheen feather from a mallard wing
Hackle: Black
Tail: Red

Teal Blue and Silver: A favourite fly of mine for many years, deadly for small school whitling at dusk in low water conditions. A size 12 is best and the slimmer it is dressed, the better.
Body: Flat silver tinsel with silver oval rib
Wings: Teal flank
Hackle: Bright blue
Tail: Golden pheasant tippet

Silver March Brown: I have known this pattern to succeed when all others have failed. Rather a nondescript fly, it may be the silver body that does the trick. Small sizes are best.
Body: Flat silver tinsel
Wings: Partridge wing
Hackle: Partridge back
Tail: Two strands as hackle

Black Pennel: Though not one of my favourites, I have included this fly because it is a very popular pattern on the lower Teifi at night and is responsible for some exceptional bags. Can be used depending on water

conditions right up to a size 2 long shank, but is probably best at size 6.
Body: Black floss ribbed oval silver tinsel
Hackle: Black
Tail: Golden pheasant tippet

Night Hawk: The only pattern that I use these days, on both dropper and
tail (I get my salmon on this one, too). Any size to suit the conditions will
catch fish. It is a Canadian pattern salmon fly and my dressing is a scaled
down version of the fully dressed fly. The butt is not essential, though I
like to incorporate it and feel that it provides an added attraction at dusk,
though possibly not after dark. Make sure that the butt is tied in neatly and
does not add bulkiness to the slimline appearance of the fly.
Body: Flat silver tinsel with silver oval rib
Wings: Black (Jungle cock, optional)
Hackle: Black
Butt: Red D.F.M. (daylight fluorescent material)
Tail: Golden pheasant crest

Peter Ross: A good fly for low water conditions when fish may be getting
stale and difficult to tempt. Fished in small sizes, 10 to 12, it sometimes
proves irresistible if 'stripped' through the water at speed in a similar
fashion to the technique used in reservoir trout fishing.
Body: Tail half flat silver tinsel, fore half red fur ribbed silver tinsel
Wings: Teal flank
Hackle: Black
Tail: Golden pheasant tippet

Hooks

I tie all my single-hook flies on fine wire low-water salmon hooks, but I
doubt whether it makes a lot of difference as to what hooks are used as long
as one or two necessary criteria are observed. A thin, needle-sharp point
with a good barb should be chosen. Whether it be down-eyed or up-eyed,
or even straight, matters little, but a small neat eye is necessary. Avoid
some of the cheaper hooks with thick metal and bulky eyes. The points on
thick wire hooks also quickly become blunt, with a resulting loss of hooking power. A good test is to press the point of the hook lightly into a piece
of varnished wood. If the point sinks in easily with light pressure and stays
put, all is well; if it falls off or needs a hard push to stay fixed, then the same
thing can happen in a fish's jaw.

In recent years the use of flies dressed on doubles and trebles has
increased. Though many anglers still stick to the single iron for all forms
of fishing, the doubles or trebles can have some advantages. Singles are
best used during the day for most conditions, but when the water is heavy
trebles can be useful to get down into the water more quickly in the faster
flow.

At night, in smaller rivers, fishing over shallow water, it is advisable to
use singles as they swim higher in the water and are less likely to pick up
debris and weed. In deeper pools or larger rivers, like the Teifi or Towy,

I use doubles or trebles which swim deeper, owing to the extra weight, and hook better when the fly is some distance away. At twenty yards distance a treble is much more likely to be driven into a firm hold than a single hook.

To be effective, flies tied on double or treble hooks must still have a slimline appearance and this is difficult on some of the short-shanked varieties. A longish shank is necessary on a treble to enable the fly to be tied properly, otherwise it has a short, stubby, unattractive look. The dressing must be tied in evenly, particularly the hackle on treble hooks, or it may be found to have an annoying slow spin when retrieved—a most undesirable feature.

The number of flies fished on a cast at any one time is a matter of personal preference or perhaps, more importantly, it depends on the expertise of the individual angler. A competent caster can quite easily handle up to three flies in the daytime, one at the tail and two droppers. The beginner would be well advised to handle one fly at a time until competent casting is achieved. If tangles do occur they can, with patience, be unravelled at the expense of lost fishing time. Not so at night, however, and much more care has to be taken. Some expert fly fishermen will habitually only use one fly at night. I use two, one dropper and one tail fly. As a general rule, I prefer two single-hook flies, but on a large river or in fairly heavy water I will opt for a double or a treble hook fly. If the flies are fairly small, say up to size 8, then two doubles can be fished or a double and a treble. If the latter combination is chosen, then the treble must be on the tail. To use two trebles is courting disaster. If choosing an elverine fly or a tube fly, it is impossible to use more than one at a time unless they are very small.

Frequent examination of the cast is necessary, especially when using multi-hook flies, to see that no knots or tangles have occurred. Trebles, in particular, tend to double back on themselves, catch the line, and fish backwards. At night, even with a good torch, bad tangles are best just rolled up and put away for sorting out later, and a new cast fitted. The most successful fifteen minutes' fishing of the trip could be lost through struggling with a difficult bird's nest.

Tube Flies

Tube fly fishing has never become popular for sea trout, as it has for salmon, except in a few localised areas. This may be due to the trend in recent decades to lighter, more versatile and more manageable tackle. Rods in particular have diminished in size to an extent that our forefathers would never have imagined. With slight variations in accompanying tackle a 9- or 10-foot rod is now used, from brown trout fishing in brooks right through to fairly heavy salmon fishing—as little as thirty years ago the latter saw fly rods of 14 and 15 feet in fairly common use.

Fishing a tube fly for sea trout requires a long rod of from 10 to 12 feet in length with a stiff action. The casting of heavy tubes is so difficult that an angler using them for the first time may find that he has to relearn his entire casting technique. They can be very useful if the water to be fished is deep and slow and it is necessary to get down to the fish. Personally, this is a method that has never appealed to me and tube flies have never been part of my armoury. Not that the method is to be shunned, for there is no doubt that on the larger rivers it is a very effective method and is responsible for some excellent catches where other methods would probably fail. The elverine or 'waddington' fly, very similar to a tube fly in the way that it fishes, is not so heavy and bulky, and is a much more interesting development than the tube. On occasions I have used these flies with some success in heavier water at night. The large flies are sometimes seized willingly by fresh-run sea trout and the bigger class of fish are certainly tempted by them. On the other hand, they are much too large for the staler fish to be interested, particularly when the water is low. Unlike tube flies that are free to slide up the line like a devon minnow, an elverine fly is dressed on a fixed body of stout wire. The bodies can be purchased separately or made up at home.

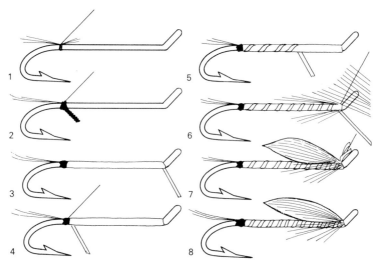

Tying a Night Hawk.

Night Fishing Preparation and Tackle

The most important item of equipment for a night fishing expedition is not an item of tackle at all, but a good torch. A small torch to carry, plus a larger one to leave in the car as a standby, is a good idea. If you happen to be one of the fortunate few who live quite close to the river and can walk to the desired fishing location then it is not essential, but if the fishing is any distance away, or a car journey is involved, a torch is a must. Alone in the early hours of the morning, miles from anywhere, perhaps in a deep gorge with rocky terrain around, a torch in the pocket is a most surprising comfort and confidence booster. Its invaluable assistance in undoing tangles, tying on flies and assessing the depth of water if it is necessary to cross from one bank to the other will be much appreciated. There are various torches on the market for the night fisherman. One is worn on the head like a miner's lamp and, though useful in leaving both hands free, is a little uncontrollable and tends to flash around needlessly. A better idea is the type with a flexible head that can be fitted to the top pocket or on the lapel. I carry a small pencil torch with me and always have a hand lantern in the car in case of emergencies. The pencil torch gives a small intense beam and can be held between the teeth to direct light downwards on to the work, leaving both hands available for the task in hand. It is important not to shine the light on the water where fishing, as this most definitely scares the fish and should be avoided at all costs. It is better to move away from the river bank and keep the light shielded from the water.

With experience it is surprising what can be done without the aid of a light. Even a blood knot can be tied in very dim light if the work is held up to the sky to show the outline. An overhand knot of fly line to a cast loop can be tied quite easily in the dark, by feel alone, with a little practice.

I carry two or three casts ready made up with flies similar to the ones I intend to use. It is then easier, when a tangle or a stubborn wind knot occurs, to take off the whole cast, roll it up and put it away for sorting out later and to fit a new one. The overhand knot is certainly bulkier than some but its simplicity is a boon when night fishing. To fit a new cast, tie an overhand knot close to the end of the fly line and pull it tight. This acts as a stopper to the second overhand knot that is passed through the cast loop and also pulled tight. Not only can the knot be easily tied by feel but it can also be undone by deftly pulling it apart with a fingernail.

It is never worth continuing to use a cast that has been badly tangled, for the monofilament is almost invariably left crinkled where it has been stretched and within a few casts the problem will occur again. The cast may also have become considerably weakened where the stretch took place. It should always be remembered that a cast is weaker than its stated strength and knots can weaken a cast by as much as 20 per cent. This is particularly true of wind knots, those annoying overhand knots that appear as if by magic, and if they are not spotted and undone, then a disaster is highly likely.

When tying knots at night it is always prudent to test with a steady pull, for one turn or hitch missed can result in the whole thing slipping loose.

Nylon monofilament It may be useful at this stage to discuss some of the properties of nylon monofilament. The only material used extensively for fishing line these days, nylon is a synthetic fibre of the 'polyamide' group. Unlike other synthetic materials, like terylene or polypropylene whose strength remains constant, nylon loses approximately 10 per cent of its strength when wet. This is the opposite to natural fibres like sisal, manila or cotton which gain strength when they are wet. Nylon also loses

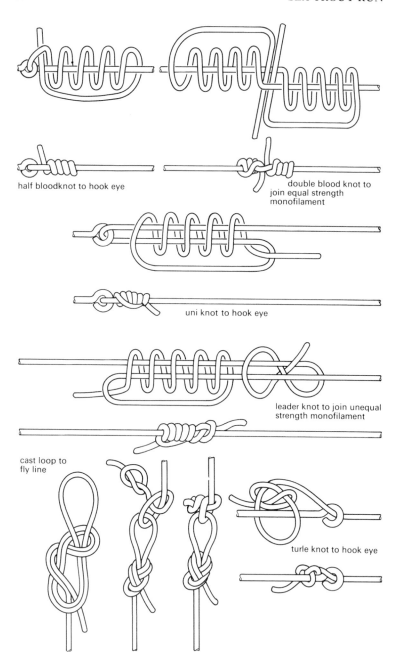

half bloodknot to hook eye

double blood knot to
join equal strength
monofilament

uni knot to hook eye

leader knot to join unequal
strength monofilament

cast loop to
fly line

turle knot to hook eye

A selection of knots

strength when exposed to sunlight over a period. It is an important point and one often overlooked. Spare spools should be stored in darkness, and never purchase any nylon from a tackle dealer's window. Even if looked after carefully, nylon deteriorates with age and after several years should be discarded or at best considered to be of somewhat less breaking strain than when it was new. Being such an important item of tackle, it is better to renew if there is any doubt.

Rods For night fishing a fairly stiff rod of 9 or 10 feet in length is adequate for all circumstances, except perhaps for fishing heavy tube flies, when something more substantial may be required.

For the beginner it would be best to choose the rod that is normally used during the day or the one found easiest to cast with, as this will prove the least difficult to master after dark. Not that there is any mysterious technique in casting after dark, but when starting it is best to use a rod that can be handled with confidence. A single-taper, floating line of the size to fit the rod will suit. Try the rod with the recommended line size and then try it with one size heavier, and see if there is any difference. Very often a rod works more positively with one size heavier line than that recommended. For instance, if the rod line size is given as an 8, try a 9; if the heavier line works better do not stick to an 8 just because the rod makers stipulate that size.

A successful evening's result on the Teifi. The scales from these fish are illustrated in the photograph on page 16.

From the fish's point of view the colour of the fly line is immaterial at night and so a very pale or white line is best so that, even in quite dark conditions, the line can be seen on the water as a guide to the position of the flies. This small point can be of real benefit when fishing in otherwise blind conditions.

Landing equipment Some means of landing the fish is necessary. If the area to be fished has shallow, gravelly beaches, then beaching, even at night, is by far the best and safest landing method. Otherwise, a landing net is the only form of suitable equipment. After dark, gaffs and tailers are better left hanging on their hooks at home where they can cause no damage. Some landing nets that are offered for sale are quite useless. The triangular folding type that clips to the belt (the only convenient thing about it) is pretty hopeless in the day time and at night can be a positive hindrance. The design of some of them is such that even if you do succeed in opening the perishing thing, the chances of getting a lively fish into it are practically nil. The most useful type is the oval-shaped, deep-netted, short-handled variety, available quite cheaply in some department stores. One word of warning, however: on the cheaper models, the rubber handle tends to pull out quite easily. If you tie a shoulder loop on the handle for ease of carrying, you may find that when you reach for the net with a good fish almost played out there is no net—it has caught on the brambles and been pulled out of the handle, and is somewhere further along the bank, out of reach.

Night Fishing Techniques

To be successful at night time fly fishing for sea trout it is necessary to know a little about their habits. These vary with the length of time that the fish have been in fresh water.

Fish which have recently entered from the sea remain active and alert throughout the day, and become even more so at dusk, just after dark, at dawn and for a short period after dawn.

After a period of seven to ten days in fresh water there is a tendency to settle down somewhat and the fish are then rarely active during the day, keeping to their chosen lies, except when a rise in water may induce them to travel further upstream. There is a period of activity from sundown, rising to a crescendo at darkness and shortly after, then an abrupt end. There is then a briefer flurry of activity in the morning between full darkness and half light. At sun up there is again an abrupt ending.

Stale sea trout that have been in the river for several weeks or even months become active only in the half-hour period before darkness in the evening and rarely show much sign of activity after that. They do not appear to show any interest in the dawn period. However, there are two exceptions to these general rules. What has been stated only applies to low water conditions. Firstly, in time of flood or heavy water the situation can become completely reversed, the sea trout being active during the day only, and at first sign of dusk all movement may cease. These conditions will provide little, if any, sport with the fly and apply more to spinning and worming. Secondly, as the season progresses and the fish are approaching spawning time the development of the gonads again moves them to activity during the day as well as at night. At this time large stale sea trout can sometimes be tempted with the fly at any time of the day or night. The ethics of taking such fish may be questionable and are best left to individual choice.

Later in the year salmon have a distinct movement pattern in heavy water and will often become active or start to move upstream in the late afternoon between three and five o'clock. I have never observed this phenomenon in sea trout, but have noticed a tendency towards upstream movement and activity in the early evening before darkness at this time of year.

Fish movement Having looked at the periods of activity it is necessary to analyse what these movements of fish can mean for the angler. Fresh fish will be cruisers and will move around a lot. In a pool they will move around the deep water, travel up to the faster water at the head and move down to the shallow water at the tail—the shallow, smooth water at the lip of the pool above the fast run into the next pool lower down. The tail of the pool is known as the 'gab' to west Wales coracle fishermen and is often the most productive area for sea trout. At any time during this cruising they can be taking fish to a large sunk fly in the deeper water, to a large floating fly at the head of the pool, or to a small floating fly at the tail.

Unlike salmon, sea trout will enter a river from the sea during periods of very low water. Under such conditions in June and July they can be seen after dark by their wakes in the shallow water, travelling up between pools.

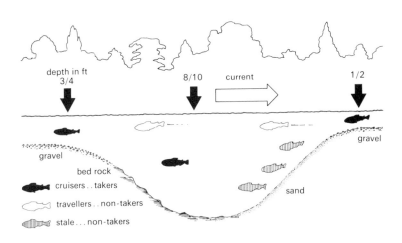

Typical pool with sea trout residents at night

Unlike the cruisers, these travellers are not taking fish and any amount of time spent casting a fly in front of their path is wasted fishing effort. They may, and probably will, become 'taking' fish when they settle down in a pool higher up.

Those that have settled in an area, and are not so intent on getting further upstream for the time being, are to be caught on the 'gab' from half light to full darkness and sometimes beyond. They will then take again as dawn approaches. These fish will lie in water so shallow it will barely cover their backs and any water deep enough to conceal a fish should not be dismissed. The head of the pool is always worth a try, that is, the shallow area just before the water deepens into the pool. This position is a favourite lie because if danger threatens from predators (including man) then a quick turn of the tail brings safer, deep water refuge.

Stale fish are rarely tempted, but may be taken at any time on the fly at night in deeper water as well as the shallow glides. However, the only really productive time for these fish is the half hour up to darkness and a little beyond.

The general rules described here will hold good at most times. There are, of course, exceptions to every rule and on the first day out a sparkling silver, fresh run sea trout of 5 lb may be caught on a tiny trout fly at 2.00 p.m. on a blazing sunny afternoon. Such is the unpredictability of angling that makes the sport all the more enjoyable and intriguing.

Weather and water conditions These can also play a most important part in night fly fishing. The best nights are those when there is a moon but overcast cloud cover. At this time, even after it has become completely dark, there is always a little light to see by, and chances are better when the floating line is visible and the position of the cast and flies can be roughly judged. Fishing blind on an overcast night with no moon in very dark conditions can be difficult unless the water is known extremely well, and pitch darkness never seems to be a good taking time anyway.

Moonlight, once the moon rises high and shines directly on the water with no tree shade, will give poor results. Fish can be caught but, owing to the light conditions, will be put off easily by the angler's movements or the splash of the line. I have never made good bags in bright moonlight.

Another poor set of conditions for night fishing is later in the year, from about mid August onwards, when the air becomes colder than the water and that strange wispy mist rises off the surface, sometimes settling in the valleys as a carpet of fog. Autumn is in the air and the fish will be getting stale. There will be no more bright-sided, sea liced and silver beauties until next year.

Do not be put off when there is thunder about, despite what some old angling stories may say. I have made some spectacular catches in the midst of a thunderstorm, not only of sea trout, but of salmon as well. The fact that it is raining also seems to make little difference, apart from the uncomfortable conditions and the difficulty in casting because of the wet line sticking to the rod rings.

For general purposes it is best to keep to a floating line. Most fishing will be done over shallow water, and a fly just under the surface, as in the so-called, greased-line salmon fishing technique, is the best. By floating fly I mean a floating line with the fly travelling just under the surface. If the fly leaves a wake there will be little success, for though there are times when sea trout, particularly fresh fish, will take a surface skidding fly, I have found that the surface disturbance deters rather than attracts them. The knot between line and cast sometimes leaves an annoying wake. To overcome the problem the plastic outer covering of the line can be lightly nicked at the knot to allow water to soak into the line's inner fibres and sink it at this point. It helps to make the flies swim just sub-surface. Some anglers may find the knot wake useful as a direction indicator, and on occasions salmon fishermen deliberately leave about a quarter of an inch of fly line at this point so that it makes a wake and therefore marks the position of the cast.

Another way to overcome the difficulty is to use a sink-tip line, although I find that it tends to sink the fly too deep with the normal 10 or 15 feet of tip. 2 or 3 feet would be ideal, but cutting a sink tip in such a way would interfere with the taper and ruin a good line.

Fishing spots Having first made sure that there are no unwanted knots on the cast and that the flies are aligned correctly, fish the near bank with a short line in the area you have chosen. Most sea trout night fishing spots are well known, especially on association water, and local knowledge or advice is helpful. If this is not forthcoming watch the local anglers and the next night, if you get to the river early enough, one of the better positions can be chosen. Very often if there is an angler fishing the opposite bank the fish, though not greatly alarmed, will have become aware of his presence and drifted over towards your bank. Stealthily fishing the near bank, therefore, can pay dividends. Only when all the water close in has been covered should a couple more yards be lengthened out to continue. Gradually covering the water by periodically lengthening the cast will ensure that no taking area is missed.

The far shore will sometimes provide takes, cast after cast. This is because the fish, not alarmed by your presence but aware of it, have moved away and have now stationed themselves on the far side of the river. In many forms of fishing, fly fishing especially, most fish are taken from the opposite bank, no matter from which side of the river the angler fishes. Vary the casts from 100° to almost 0°, that is, from 10° upstream of directly across to almost straight below. Each cast will present the fly to the fish from a different aspect. When casting across the main current the line tends to belly downstream and the speed of the fly increases as it swings round. This is the situation where, when fishing in the daytime, particularly for salmon, it is necessary to mend the line upstream to steady the movement of the fly. Fishing at the tail of a pool in fairly shallow water is no place to start line mending, especially if the water surface is smooth. The disturbance will cause fish to move away into deeper water, so line

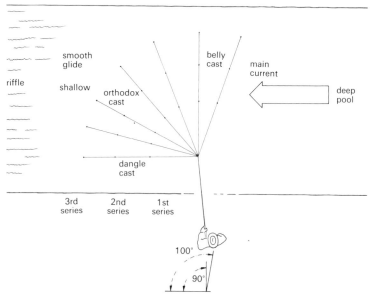

Fly fishing—covering the tail of a pool

mending should be reserved for the rougher stretches of water, and these are only worth fishing during the day. For some reason, the whip round of the fly when the line bellies on the water proves attractive to sea trout at night and sometimes they will take it when the fly is literally racing downstream through the water. The fish has sighted the fly near the far bank, and though not tempted at first, it sees this apparently live object darting away and will chase and seize it before it is lost.

When fishing the cast out, it is always best to leave it on the dangle downstream for a few seconds and then slowly retrieve a few yards. This again is a good taking time, especially if the water has not been disturbed by wading and there are some rocks or overhanging bushes below, under which the fish may be lying.

In certain conditions fish will prefer an almost stationary fly to one that is being pulled in fast, so while covering the water it pays to vary the technique until the right formula is found. As a rule, fresh fish will take a fly moving rapidly close to the surface over shallow water. As they settle in the river, fishing deeper water with less movement and allowing the fly to sink a little can prove successful.

The Take The take itself can vary from a vicious tug to a gentle hold, and on odd occasions nothing is felt at all as a fish takes the fly and swims towards the rod. Unlike salmon fishing, a strike is always necessary when sea trout fishing at night. This can be a difficult art to master and only comes with experience because the strength of the cast, the stiffness of the rod, the distance from the fish and the angler's own reactions all play a part. The strike should be more of a deliberate slow pull rather than a strike. This will set the hook hold. At night sea trout will sometimes take the fly gently and, immediately on feeling a strange hard object, release it. If take after take occurs like this and no fish are hooked, there is a need to vary the striking technique to meet the situation. It must be immediate but not hard. The tendency is to get all keyed up in anticipation and then, if a light take occurs, the resulting snatch will hook the fish, but the fish will have the fly in its jaw and the angler will be left having to tie on another. A curse or two may help to relieve the disappointment, but there is no shame involved for it is the commonest way to lose fish and fly as any reservoir fisherman will also vouch.

There is also the all too frequent occasion, particularly when the school whitling are about, when take after take results in nothing being hooked. No amount of technique changes can overcome the problem as the fish are just tweaking at the tail of the fly and avoiding the barb. The one remedy is to change to a smaller fly—sometimes a very small trout fly will prove the only answer.

Cast strength Cast strength will be governed by the water conditions and in general the lower the water the finer it is necessary to fish. Anything less than 5 lb breaking strain is taking needless risks, however, especially when large fish are likely to be encountered. I use an 8 lb cast when fishing heavier water, or early in the season when strong fish are about, and then fine down to 6 lb later in the year for low water conditions. A tapered cast can be most helpful in that it does make casting easier and gives a better fly presentation. A good idea is to use about 3 feet of 15 or 20 lb monofilament between fly line and cast.

The length of cast needs to be as long as possible without being unwieldy. A 10-foot rod with a cast of the same length is ideal. If it is longer it is necessary to make sure that the line-to-cast knot can pass through the top ring easily, otherwise a fish may be lost at the last moment on a short line near the net.

Unless it is necessary, for example, to reach a certain productive stretch of water, avoid wading in the dark. Not only is it dangerous, especially on larger rivers if the water is not known very well indeed, but it also frightens the fish. It is most difficult to wade without disturbing the water and stumbling over stones, causing vibrations that the fish will sense and become alarmed about. On many occasions I have carefully approached a favourite spot to find an angler standing in the water at the very place, or sometimes even beyond, where I would expect fish to be taken. Wading spoils the fishing for the angler concerned and, more importantly, for the one who follows, probably for the remainder of that night.

Day Fly Fishing Techniques

Fly fishing for sea trout in the daytime, with a few exceptions, can be a very unproductive and frustrating angling method. This is the case for most of England and Wales, where possibly over 90 per cent of all the sea trout caught on a fly are caught at dusk or after dark. The two notable exceptions are in Ireland and the north of Scotland, particularly the Shetland Isles. Being fortunate enough to be able to fish for sea trout over a period of weeks in Galway and County Mayo in the summers of 1970 and 1971, I grasped the challenge from local anglers who said that I would not be able to catch any sea trout, or white trout as they are called in Ireland, on a fly at night. They were right and, after several abortive attempts, I gave up. The most productive time in night fishing is when the water is quite clear. In Ireland the water in most rivers is the colour of beer, even in low flows, caused by the drain off from peat bogs. This could be the reason for the lack of sport at night; at least it is the only explanation that I can think of. In the daytime, however, many sea trout are caught on the fly, especially loch fishing from boats. On some of these lochs, like Loch Furnace in County Mayo, sea trout are caught at all times of the day, even on bright sunny days, provided there is a breeze to ripple the surface.

The other well-known daytime sea trout fishing is in the voes and sea lochs of Shetland and the Faroes, where fast and furious sport may be obtained among the shoals of sea trout in late summer. As far as I know this is also the only area of the country where sea trout can be regularly fished for and caught in salt water. The occasional fish is caught in an estuary or on the coast by an angler fishing for bass or bottom fishing for cod, but this is very much the exception rather than the rule.

The best daytime fly fishing is after a spate when the water has cleared off sufficiently for the fish to be able to see the fly. A good guide is when the bottom stones can be seen at a depth of two feet. For water any dirtier than this spinning should be the order of the day.

Shallow runs If there are fresh fish in the river, then it is always a sound idea to fly fish in the shallow, fast runs. Sea trout, particularly when fresh in from the sea, like to lie in fast-flowing, sometimes almost white, well oxygenated water and, provided there is a little cover such as an overhanging tree, a high bank or some boulders, will quite happily lie in two feet of water or even less. Fish a wet fly on a floating line across and downstream, letting the flies hang or falter for a moment, if possible, behind rocks and in the slacker patches of water.

It has been suggested in the past that dry fly fishing is a good method of fishing for sea trout. They can be caught on a dry fly, without doubt, but unless you wish to experiment this form of fishing is best left to the trout fishermen and the chalk streams.

Fast runs When fly fishing in fast water and runs, remember the taking places, for although sea trout are not quite like salmon in that they do not occupy known lies, except perhaps for the larger fish, the resting places will nevertheless remain in similar spots year after year. Once a good sea trout taking place has been discovered, it will, as a rule, continue to produce fish unless the bottom and/or current configuration changes.

It is often said that a 'lady's' salmon rod or a grilse rod of about eleven feet is ideal for sea trout. This is most certainly true of heavy water and larger rivers, but for normal sea trout fishing a stiff 'reservoir' rod that can handle an 8 line is ample. The line can be of any colour, even white, and should be a double-taper floater. If a sinking line is preferred, then a rod strong enough to lift the line out of the water is needed. However, I see little use in a sinking line for sea trout fishing except for one or two specialised methods. The cast should be as light as one dare use with confidence. 6 lb breaking strain is the best for general use, but even down to 4 lb will pay dividends in very low, clear water conditions. When fishing so fine for such a vigorous fighting fish, it must be remembered that the knot strength reduces the breaking strain even further and that fish must be hooked and played with care. Unlike fishing at night, a strike is not really needed and fish will hook themselves, if given a little slack, in a similar fashion to that most self-disciplined art of salmon fly fishing—give slack and allow the hook to pull into the angle of the jaw. A fly fisherman who has had fine sport the night before and landed several good fish by mastering the knack of a short sharp strike, who has a good rise the next morning and does not, at the very least, twitch the wrist, is a man of admirable self-restraint. Very often, especially in fast water during the day, the first knowledge of a take is that a fish is being played, there being no intermediate period in which to think about whether to strike or not.

Playing Fish on the Fly

Playing fish on the fly is a technique that develops with experience and, as long as a few basic rules are observed, can be learned fairly quickly. The rod needs to be light and springy for casting and this also helps when playing the fish. Avoid a rod that bends markedly from tip to butt, the only springiness should be in the top section, with little or no bend between ferrule and reel. The top section is, and should be, used as a shock absorber to cushion heavy or violent pulls on the line which would otherwise break the light cast.

The reel should be full to just below the brim, with at least fifty yards of backing. The backing is necessary for, on occasions, large fish which have no intentions of remaining in the immediate vicinity will be encountered. This is particularly true of bigger, wider waters. Once, fishing an Irish loch with light tackle, I had a fresh sea trout of 4 lb take a hundred yards of backing to the reel knot before I managed to persuade him to turn, and even then I suffered both waders filling with water. On small streams this is very unlikely to happen unless the water is heavy and the fish decides that it would be better off back in the sea, which they are sometimes prone to do. If a fish runs, hold the rod up and allow the reel to release line, running with the ratchet on. An overrun now will prove disastrous. When it turns, retrieve line as it swims towards the rod. The advantage of a full reel then becomes plain, as far fewer turns are necessary to retrieve line than with a reel that is almost empty.

The trick is to keep the same or a similar amount of strain on the fish at all times when playing it. Some time spent in watching a coarse fisherman playing a large bream or carp on 2 lb line would be well worthwhile.

Although sea trout can be much more violent in their runs and jumps, the technique is basically the same. If the fish jumps, as sea trout often do, lower the rod tip to allow for any sudden jerk or snatch on the cast. This is a similar reaction to a motorist who counter-steers into a skid, and once learned is done instinctively.

There are two basic methods of playing a fish. Assuming that the angler is right-handed, on hooking a fish the rod is passed to the left hand and the reel is controlled with the right. Line is allowed to be pulled off the reel by the fish or retrieved, as required. The other method, though much more untidy and dangerous from the point of view of losing the fish, is favoured by many anglers. This is to keep the rod in the right hand and to manipulate the line unreeled in a pile on the bank when pulling a fish in and letting it run out when the fish swims away.

An intermediate solution, and a compromise between the two methods, is to keep the rod in the right hand for the initial few hard runs, then, when the fish has tired somewhat, to change hands, reel in the surplus line and finish playing the fish with the rod in the left hand and the right hand to the reel. This is the method used by a number of anglers. It also means that when the fish is played out, the right hand is free to use whatever landing gear is employed. These are not hard and fast rules but will help the angler to choose the best method according to his own skill and preference. If it comes naturally, then all the better—after all, many anglers are as unaware of which hand holds the rod when playing a good fish as they are of changing from third to top gear when travelling to work in the car.

When a fish is nearing the stage at which it will soon be ready for landing there are several pitfalls to guard against. On hooking a fish the experienced angler will have automatically made a mental note of the best spot for landing it. If there is a shingle beach close by, then this is by far the safest bet. When the fish is so weakened that it lays on its side (beware a second wind), guide it slowly but firmly into shallow water to the shore. As it hits the beach it will probably kick once or twice, which will only serve to strand it higher. There is then a knack, quickly perfected, of getting between the fish and the water's edge, grasping the tail wrist, and pushing the fish up the beach. Do not attempt to lift it up by the tail while it is still in or close to the water.

If a landing net is being used, there are three golden rules to observe for a disaster to be avoided. The first is never attempt to land a fish that is still fighting; the second, is to submerge the net completely and draw the fish over it and then lift; the third, if it is a large fish, is to get it in the net head first.

In the later stages of playing a fish beware of the line-to-cast knot becoming caught in the top ring. If using a dropper, keep a watchful eye out for driftwood, weed or debris on which the trailing fly may catch. Landing nets especially have a nasty habit of catching on to any loose flies hanging about and are the cause of many a lost fish.

Lastly, land your own fish if you can, for, after all, it is an integral part of the sport of angling. A fish lost at the net can ruin a lifelong friendship; I never land another person's fish unless specifically asked to do so.

8
Spinning

Spinning for sea trout can be the most rewarding of all angling experiences and some anglers who habitually seek the species use no other method. The term spinning is not strictly correct for, though many years ago the spinning devon minnow was used almost exclusively, today there are many different sorts of lures used in the same manner. Spinning could be said to include the use of any artificial bait which is cast out and then retrieved with a view to enticing a fish to seize it.

Types of Spinner

The Devon Minnow There is now a large choice in spinners and lures. The old devon minnow which was designed to resemble a small fish is still used extensively in various forms. The bull nose devon went through a phase of high popularity in the 'fifties and is, even now, still preferred by some die-hard devon stalwarts. Another favourite, still sometimes used, is the flat-sided, reflex devon. Wooden devons have become extremely popular in recent years, especially for salmon. They are fished with a weight on the line above, which, when pulled across close to the bottom, leaves the buoyant wooden minnow to wave and hover enticingly behind.

Devon minnows can be armed with a single treble at the tail, two trebles in tandem, one behind the other, or be of the side-hook, slotted variety with an additional treble mounted on each side. The side-hook devon is particularly good at hooking sea trout owing to the tendency of these fish to seize the bait from the side.

Releasing a small sea trout with a mouth full of four trebles, however, can be a harrowing experience to an angler with arthritic fingers, not to mention the discomfort the fish will experience. In some areas these multi-hook weapons are banned. Devons can be made of a number of materials: steel, brass, lead, plastic, or wood which is the commonest, or a combination of one or more of these. Like flies, some are painted and designed to catch the angler's eye rather than the fish's and for sea trout the brighter shades of yellow, red, blue and green should generally be avoided, with silver, gold, black or brown preferred. Completely silver is probably the best all-round colour available, with gold a good second best. That is not to say that some colours or patterns do not catch fish; some colours and sizes, however, will catch fish consistently better than others.

The preference may vary from river to river and visiting anglers would be well advised to seek local knowledge as to the best choice of lure. General rules which can be applied are that the heavier and dirtier the water, the brighter and larger the spinner needs to be, whereas in lower and clearer water, a duller and smaller spinner is best.

Speed of retrieve is also important with devons, and in heavy water they should be spun slowly and allowed to 'hang' in the current as much as possible. In low, clear conditions they need to be spun quickly and in very clear conditions as fast a retrieve as the angler can make is still not too fast for a determined fish to give chase and catch its prey.

The Quill Similar to the devon minnow, but not quite in the same category, is the quill, which deserves its own separate description. These baits can be deadly for sea trout when spun fast downstream in clear water. They seem to inspire a particular attraction, possibly because they closely resemble small fish with their semi-transparent bodies. Their disadvantage is that they are light and sometimes do not spin well unless retrieved very quickly, and almost invariably the trebles fitted to shop-bought ones are too small. It is amazing how on occasion a sea trout is seen to take the whole lure into its mouth and then spit it out without being hooked. Unless they are home-made (the parts can sometimes be bought from tackle dealers), when a suitably large tail treble can be fixed, there is no alternative possible for the trebles cannot be changed without a complete strip-down and rebuild of the minnow.

A type of devon minnow known as the 'Irish' or 'Lane' minnow has recently become available. This is proving to be very popular with sea trout anglers and has a transparent look about it similar to a quill minnow. They are made of plastic, have slim lines and have a lead core to provide the casting weight.

Spoons Spoons are another type of spinner that have been used in angling for a very long time. Over the years they have been liked by pike and perch anglers, and are also used for catching various species of sea fish. They have now, however, become one of the most favoured baits for sea trout, with the 'mepps' type proving the most popular choice. It is made of a spoon-shaped blade fitted to a clevis which revolves around a central wire at a nicely even and uniform rate. Uneven spinning, which can spoil its attraction, is caused by the clevis closing up to jam partially the free running of the blade, the central wire support being bent or the spoon blade itself being bent or misshapen. These spoons are numbered from one to five, the low numbers being the smallest. Sizes two and three in the middle range are the best for sea trout.

They can be purchased in various colours, different coloured spots being the favoured design but, as with devon minnows, a plain silver is probably the best all-rounder, particularly in heavy water when most spinning takes place anyway. In clear water a plain gold spoon, or a dark bronze, is sometimes effective. Very often it is the older ones that have become tarnished with age which the fish seem to prefer.

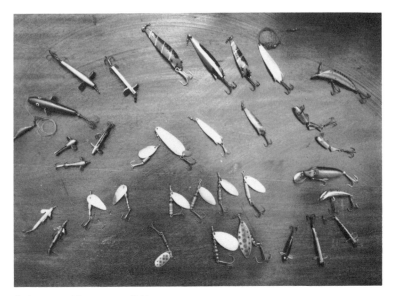

Spinners used in sea trout fishing

Different types of landing gear

The shape of these spoons varies from almost round to oval, and some are even pear-shaped. The elongated oval, sometimes referred to as the 'long' type, is by far the best for sea trout fishing, especially in small, fast streams. On bigger, deeper waters the spoon shape is not so important and then any shape to suit individual preference can be chosen. The long blade slips through the water more easily and quickly than a round one which produces more water resistance, enabling it to be spun more slowly and made to hang better in the current.

On some of these spinners the hooks supplied are too small and of poor quality and should be changed. If the existing treble is snipped free at the edge of the eye and a small split ring fitted, the spinner can be armed with another more suitable treble (usually one size larger) which can easily be replaced if it becomes blunt or broken. The fitting of a split ring also serves one other useful purpose. It extends the hang of the treble by that extra few millimetres, which increases the chances of hooking the fish that comes a little short.

Another type of spoon popular a few years ago, but rarely seen today, is the 'vibro'. This spoon has no clevis, the central wire passing through a hole at the top of the spoon blade. It gave an irregular action which can best be described as a fluttering motion, very like the struggles of an injured fish. This is probably what makes it so attractive to sea trout and it is well worth a try in heavy, coloured water.

DIY Spoons Both the aforementioned types of spoon can be made at home by the handyman angler with a few basic tools such as a vice and a pair of strong pliers. Some tackle manufacturers will supply the materials that are needed or, if they are hard to obtain, it is surprisingly easy for a friend who works in an engineering shop to punch out some really good blades once provided with a pattern. One of the advantages of making them at home is that the body can be weighted as required, not to mention the considerable saving on expense. Hanging spinners on trees, a favourite pastime of some anglers, can be heartbreakingly expensive, but if they are home-made, the wrench on the pocket is not quite so severe. As with home-tied flies, the catch of a good fish on a bait made by oneself has that certain extra ingredient of satisfaction.

Bar spoons like the 'toby' have become very popular in recent years. Their action is most enticing even when retrieved very slowly, and they are available in a wide range of sizes, shapes, weights and colours. They do not spin but wobble from side to side when drawn through the water, owing to their bent and uneven shape. These lures are particularly good for large early run sea trout in May and June in a fining off flood. Monocolour silver is the best all-rounder, with brown and gold a close second choice.

On some types the fitted treble is too small and one larger should be substituted—an easy task, for most are already fitted with a split ring. The silver tinned hooks sometimes supplied with them have poor hooking powers, the point not being sharp enough and too easily blunted. Change them.

For sea trout fishing the bar spoon has become notorious for fish losses after apparently secure hooking. This is probably due to the wobbling motion which sometimes causes the fish to miss or not seize the lure properly. There is also a large amount of body for the fish to grasp without coming into contact with the treble hook at the tail. What appears to be a solid take does nothing more than dent a few teeth on the fish's part and provoke muttered profanities from the angler. Fixing a smaller treble to the side of the lure by drilling a small hole and fitting a split ring can overcome the problem to a certain extent, and will result in fish being hooked more securely. Care should be taken that this does not interfere with the bait's action in the water; it should be loose and jumpy, and should not have a sliding motion.

Plugs are another type of lure that are widely used, especially for pike, and they are great favourites in North America for such fresh water fish as the small-mouth bass. In that country they come in hundreds of different shapes and sizes. They are normally shaped to wriggle through the water and can be fitted with various sorts of vane to make them dive or swim near the surface, whichever is preferred. They can be made of wood or plastic and, less often, metal. A few years ago a plug called the 'Canadian Wiggler' enjoyed some success with sea trout anglers in south Wales. There are other well tried varieties but plug fishing for sea trout is not popular and is a method rarely employed. A small type of plastic, transparent, jointed wriggler which is really a plug can sometimes be successful in small, fast rivers in clear water.

Spinning in Heavy Water

Spinning is a very popular method of sea trout fishing, and never more so than after a summer flood when more fish are caught than at any other time. Unlike worm fishing where the bait flows in a more or less straight line downstream, or even remains stationary and relies on the fish to find it, a spinner is continually covering new water. In a reasonably short space of time a whole area of river can be covered to such an extent that any fish lying in the vicinity will have seen the bait at least once and been given the opportunity to take it if it feels so inclined. Even when fly fishing, which is not normally practised in heavy, coloured water, the bait is somewhat restricted in its presentation in that areas of the stream quite close to where the angler may be fishing are not covered, particularly upstream and across from where he stands.

This advantage of being able to cover all the likely water while spinning means that if there is a taking fish within range, then there is every chance that the bait will be presented to it at some time or other.

Summer floods Good spinning water does not, however, happen very frequently, for it is always associated with a rise in the river and accompanying coloured water conditions. With the unpredictable British weather a summer flood may occur a dozen times during the sea trout season from May to September, or in some years may not happen at all.

During the summer, especially May and June, there is so much water taken up by plant growth, in addition to evaporation, that a considerably greater amount of rain is required for a summer flood to produce bank high conditions than in the winter when the ground is already sodden and there is no growth or evaporation taking place.

Summer floods usually occur when a depression has moved in from the west and a resulting warm front has produced steady rain for at least six hours (less if another front has produced appreciable rain in the preceding twenty-four hours). Thunderstorms also produce floods but of a different nature. They tend to be sudden, with a very fast rise of the rivers making them unusually muddy and laden with debris, and therefore unfishable for several hours. Thunderstorm floods tend to run off quickly and within a day the river may drop to its pre-flood, low water condition. Such flash floods do not draw many fish in from the sea, and in some instances can result in the residents of a particular stretch moving upstream and no fish coming in to replace them.

Rising water is not normally any good for spinning (or for any other method for that matter), but there are one or two exceptions to this rule. In July and August when there are generally a good number of fish in the river, which have possibly pushed up from the estuary with the high tides and moved upstream at night, the first of a rise can pay dividends. The fish will know by the amount of rain that has fallen if there is a flood to come. After a couple of hours of steady rain the river will not have risen but will be just slightly tinted from road gutters and farm yards. The freshening of water can wake up the fish to such an extent that they will even begin to travel upstream. Almost invariably it means fishing in the rain, but to offset that discomfort there may be a short period, possibly less than half an hour, when they will strike a small mepps or devon quite freely. I remember the time when the weather made no difference whatsoever to my angling pleasure but as the years go by I must admit I have less and less desire to venture out with the rod in inclement weather, unless the prospects are exceedingly good. I am still sorely tempted on occasions such as this. As soon as the real rise begins, water colouring rapidly and weed and twigs beginning to move, sport will cease. For some reason all interest in a bait will come to an abrupt ending, even though a few fish will still be travelling.

Polluted water In an identical situation after a prolonged spell of dry weather and low water, there will be no sport at all. This is when sudden heavy rain washes the road drains into the river, containing miniscule particles of tyre rubber, oil and all the associated nasties attached to modern civilisation. The tainted river will cause an uncomfortable period for the sea trout, until the rising water dilutes the pollutants, and there will be no interest shown in any baits. In extreme cases these particular conditions have been known to cause fish deaths. Another situation where fish may take in rising water is in the event of a second flood shortly after the first. When a flood has brought in fresh fish from the sea and then the river has fallen until they no longer show any interest in a lure, they may come to life and start taking again as rain causes the river to rise a second time. Much of the muddy debris-laden water which the fish so dislike will have washed away with the first rise.

Even in summer it is amazing what a river will wash down when it rises into flood after heavy rain. Grass, leaves, twigs and weed, not to mention dead animals which have fallen in or even been thrown in and all sorts of questionable rubbish, joins the water in its unending journey to the sea. Sea trout dislike such conditions and very often cease to travel on rising water because of them. Instead they sit tight in eddies and backwaters until the water is of a healthier composition.

The waters will rise for several hours, depending on the amount of rain that has fallen and how dry the land was to begin with. The rate of increase slows down as the flood reaches its full height. The maximum level will hold for an hour or so, rarely more than two, and then it will slowly start to drop. The colour of the muddy water and the amount of debris in it decrease towards the top of the flood, and once it starts to drop the leaves and sticks will slowly diminish. Sea trout now begin to run if the water flow is not too heavy and turbulent, and the worm fishermen will have begun in earnest. The spinner will have to wait yet awhile.

Level marker If a stretch of water is fished regularly, it is most useful to have some sort of level marker so that all the stages of the river's rise and fall can be instantly noted. A plank marked off in inches with white paint, standing in the margins somewhere and bolted to a tree or wall tells at a glance what is happening to the level. Water Authority engineers are helpful in often placing such gauges in convenient places, but they are always in metres, decimetres and centimetres these days, which we will all have to get used to sooner or later! Those experienced in river craft can recognise the rises from signs of straining water tension on the dry stones or the packing of leaves against bankside stones and obstructions. The tell-tale signs of falling water are grass, exposed but still bent, debris tidelines or the distinctive wet ribbon on stones just above the water line.

Time to spin Precisely when to start spinning is a problem to which there is no definite answer. It is amazing how sea trout are able to see and seize a spinner in quite muddy water. Perhaps it is better to begin before conditions look right, rather than later. If an object can be seen in the water at three to four inches' depth, then it is well worth a try, but while the river is dirty and heavy only the shallow, slower areas are likely to produce a fish. It is necessary to retrieve at a very slow rate and, where possible, to allow the spinner to hang in the current, as a fish will sometimes take when the bait is quite stationary. Fish are likely to take right at the angler's feet and on occasions will seize the spinner just as it is about to be lifted from the surface. For this reason the cast should be fished out deliberately and slowly to the bankside. There is no point whatsoever in the often seen practice of throwing the bait to the far bank when the current is too strong and turbulent for fish to lie in midstream.

They will be lying in the quieter side waters and those are the areas that should be covered.
A bright silver bait is the best for such conditions, and it should be a size or two larger than is normally preferred. In such water the largest size of mepps or toby available will catch whitling since, with visibility so poor, a very large bait is the one that is going to be seen. The next choice of colour, oddly enough, should be black. It is almost certainly the case that fish only see a black outline from below anyway and are unable to pick up the actual colour unless looking at it from the side. Using a black or dark-coloured spinner, therefore, accentuates the bait in poor water visibility. The black and brown coloured toby is particularly good in this type of fishing. As a rule, fast retrieve is the order of the day for sea trout, but here a slow one is essential. The fish may only see the bait for a split second and must have time to move and grab it before it disappears from view. For this reason a fish hooked is often well hooked and will sometimes have taken the spinner well down into the throat. They only get one chance and make the most of it.

As the river starts to drop and the current settles down to a steadier rate, the length of cast can be extended to cover more water as the fish spread out across the river. Size of spinner now needs to be scaled down accordingly, since one too large will have the opposite effect and scare fish away. The smooth runs at the tail of the pools should be covered thoroughly. Fish will be travelling and, after struggling up through the rough rapid water, they will pause on the gab for a while for a breather before moving into the deeper water of the pool. These will be taking fish just to the side of the main current flow. Direction of cast and speed of retrieve can now be varied and it is necessary to fish to the very lip where the smooth water falls away to the rapids below.

The water will still be so heavy as to provide a run in almost any section of the cast, but several well defined areas where they are most likely to be can be pinpointed. Having cast over the main current to the far bank, the first optimum point is as the spinner just comes into the main current flow, beginning to accelerate diagonally downstream. There is a knack of allowing the spinner to pause momentarily at this point by slowing the wind and lifting the rod tip slightly. The second optimum point is as the spinner leaves the main current on the angler's side and is swinging round to start being retrieved upstream. From here to the rod tip a take is likely.

It is worth drawing the spinner slowly across at the very tip of the gab and repeating this cast at frequent intervals. The lip of a water fall can be an excellent taking place and often a run will occur so near to the edge that before the angler realises what is happening the fish is over and into the pool below.

Coverage of water Every possible area of fish-holding water should be explored, moving about from place to place, but it must always be remembered that fish will be moving about also and what may be an unproductive spot once may yield a fish later. If fish are known to be running, many anglers prefer to stay in one place, covering the same water continuously. This method tends to be rather monotonous but it can certainly pay off, especially when salmon fishing, for sooner or later a taking fish is likely to come along. Sea trout, however, tend to spread out over the river and it may be better to move about looking for good taking places. If a spot is found where a fish is caught or a run occurs, it is worth while trying in the same place again after a short rest. Other fish may have moved in or the fish that struck at the lure the first time round will make the fatal mistake at the second invitation. A sea trout will sometimes strike at a lure and miss and then come a second time with more deliberation and get hooked, either on the same cast or successive ones.

A run will not produce a fish on each occasion now, as it did earlier on. Good, hard knocks will result in no fish being hooked and frequently there will be a flash or surface boil, with no contact made whatsoever. Fish may be lost while being played, some after only a second or two and some, most frustratingly, just before they are ready to be landed. An average of one fish to every four runs can be regarded as quite a reasonable score.

What can often be most annoying is when a couple of good fish make an attempt to seize one of the swivels as they furrow through the surface. A fly will do the trick you say? It will not—it is still too heavy and dirty. A dodge used by some is to tie a fly or even a bare hook to the swivel. This only encourages fish to go for it and is also illegal. Swivels can play an important part in that they may attract the attention of the fish as they go by but, not being of any size or significance, the fish allows them past with only a cursory glance. It is, however, alerted and when the spinner following on behind comes into view it is seized by an already interested fish poised to strike.

Frustration can set in, even among experienced anglers, if four or five good fish are lost in a row and when the cursing starts perhaps it is better to resort to a beer and the television rather than increase the blood pressure. I always compare heavy-water sea trout spinning with a lucky (or unlucky) run at cards. How often in an evening of bridge or solo does one constantly get good or bad cards? Is there such a thing as a run of luck? All I know is that sometimes fish after fish is lost and at other times almost every run results in a fish on the bank.

As the water drops even more and begins to clear so that the gravel can be seen at depths of a foot or so, the pool tails and smoother glides should be left and the faster runs and riffles given a try. Water of an even depth of three to four feet and travelling at a fast walking pace is the ideal sea trout run. Even if the water looks too fast and turbulent at the surface there may be quiet water near the bottom where fish will lie quite happily. At this time it is better to have some form of set approach rather than just walking along the bank casting here, there and everywhere. Whether one starts at the top of a run and fishes down or starts at the bottom and works up is really immaterial. Generally, I like to start at the top if the water is very heavy and coloured and at the bottom if the water is lower and clearer with, perhaps, the odd fish being frightened by my presence. At the starting point, say, where deep rough water shallows out into the run, throw a series of casts varying from across and just upstream to almost below, like a fan formation. Having completed this series, move downstream (or upstream) about five yards and carry out the same sequence as before. Quartering the water in such a way means that all likely fish lies are systematically covered. Continue downstream until reaching the gab or the beginning of deeper water into the next pool. The whole process can then start again or, alternatively, if a fish has been caught or seen in a particular spot, which will have been noted by marking with a bush, tuft of grass or stone, it will be worthy of more efforts.

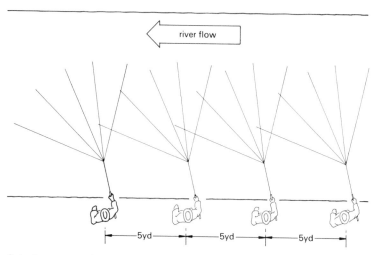

Spinning—quartering a run

Good runs Those anglers who fish a stretch of water season after season get to know where the best places are. Certain pool tails and runs will produce fish consistently whereas areas of a similar nature that look to be good taking places will rarely, if ever, produce fish. A spot that has proved productive in one flood will probably do the same in the next and subsequent floods. When fishing a new water it can sometimes pay to make a short note of the taking places. A run counts as much as a fish grassed, for each could easily have been reversed. Such a note might say that a fish was caught beneath the sycamore bush at the railway pool with the river level at x inches, heavy and coloured, fallen four inches, time, date, etc., and can be made up of as much comprehensive information as each individual wishes. Under similar conditions, perhaps the following year, the chances of meeting a fish at that place are high. The making of such notes for future reference can be invaluable, especially if the type of lure used and its size are also recorded. If a brown and gold devon of two inches did the trick once it is most certainly capable of doing it again. The same principles apply to fly fishing or worming and, for that matter, to any form of fishing.

While the fishing is good it pays to make the most of it, so cut chatting time to fellow anglers to a minimum. There will be time enough to describe the loss of the big one that rushed off downstream and took your devon with him when the taking period is over, as it will be all too soon. Do not wait for another angler to move from a good spot; search around, for in this water there will be fish spread about the river in areas that are quickly vacated in lower water.

This period of good fishing will come to an abrupt end when the colour of the water turns to that of dark beer and the bottom stones can be seen at eighteen inches to two feet. Depending on the size of the initial flood, the spinning water will have lasted anything from two to six hours. It also depends on the size of the river, because small streams may only produce the ideal conditions for an hour or so while larger rivers can remain in form for most of the day. On most rivers land drainage works have ensured that flood water runs off quickly, and the spinning period is considerably reduced from what it was a number of years ago.

Spinning in Low Water

Spinning in low water, though nothing like as productive as after a flood, can nevertheless pay dividends under certain conditions. All the precautions that are necessary for low, clear water fishing need to be observed, such as a careful and steady approach to the riverside (at a crouch if necessary), dull, unobtrusive clothing and every effort made to keep out of sight.

There are three main areas of approach to clear water sea trout spinning: in the early morning just after dawn; fishing runs and fast riffles; and spinning upstream.

When the water is clear in July and August and there are fresh-run fish moving into the pools, especially in the lower reaches just above the tide, there is always the chance of a fish at first light. Some will have moved up during the night and will not yet have settled in the pools or become fully accustomed to their new, fresh water environment. These fish will not have seen any of the angling activity of the day before and will be taking fish if approached in the right way.

Method A small mepps or devon is the preferred method, for it is necessary to spin fairly fast, and a wobbling spoon or plug will tend to scare the fish rather than attract them. Move in an upstream direction, approaching pools and runs from below and casting across and upstream into the deeper water, drawing the lure fast and steadily into shallow water. In this kind of fishing, unlike almost any other, the fish will be seen following the lure, striking at it, sometimes missing it, even circling round and coming in for another go.

Whatever happens it is essential to keep on retrieving at the same rate without hesitation and not be tempted to slow down to enable the fish to catch up. If the fish wishes to seize it then it will do so, being able to travel faster than any speed at which an angler can retrieve. A fish will sometimes follow the bait to the very feet of the angler and when this happens it is imperative to keep absolutely still, apart from the hand winding the reel, and fish the cast right out.

If several fish can be seen in a pool and they have not previously been disturbed or seen the angler's approach, they may turn in unison towards

The author with a three-and-a-half pounder, fresh from the tide

the lure and follow it. A very high degree of casting accuracy is required, since it is on the first cast that there is a 90 per cent chance of a fish seizing the bait. The second cast uses up virtually the whole of the remaining 10 per cent, and after that there is little chance of the fish taking any notice at all. Just a handful of casts in each likely place is all that is necessary before moving on. If a fish is caught, then it normally disturbs the area and you should proceed to the next likely hole. This type of angling is very much a 'first-come, first-served' affair, for if any angler has covered the water before, or if a return to cover the water again is made, it is most unlikely that a fish will move to the bait.

When first arriving at the water do not be tempted to fish until it is quite light, since sea trout are poor spinner-takers in the early dawn gloom. The fifteen to twenty minutes before sun-up are the best, or sometimes even later. The most essential ingredient is that nothing has disturbed the water. A cormorant, low flying heron, fluttering moorhen or a farmyard dog walking the bank can all put the fish down as far as that particular piece of water is concerned.

Fishing fast runs and riffles at any time of the day can be worthwhile if there are fresh fish in the river and the water has not been disturbed too much. This method is sometimes very effective for fresh whitling. Fast, rough water of a couple of feet in depth, particularly if it is interspersed with boulders or quieter patches, is ideal holding water. It is always worth remembering that the current at the bottom is never the same as at the top and what may look like an impossibly fast flow may hold fish quite comfortably. It is relatively easy to see fish in a couple of feet of smooth, clear water, but the same depth of fast riffle makes it impossible because of the surface agitation. The same is true of the angler on the bank from the fishes' point of view, for broken water also shields the angler from the fish.

Covering the water 'Stickles' under low-hanging trees and banks are favourite lies and every likely place should be explored—it is amazing where a sea trout will appear. Using a small mepp, preferably dull gold or tarnished, vary the cast across and up, and alter the speed of retrieve to allow the lure to hang momentarily behind rocks and obstructions. It is necessary to fish the cast out right to the water's edge, because sometimes a fish may sight the lure at the far bank and follow it all the way across the river. At other times there will be a wild snatch as the bait passes through the fish's window of vision. As in all clear water fishing it is better to work upstream, covering the runs from the lower end upwards. It is rarely worth lingering over the deeper, slower waters.

The last, and most exciting, of clear water methods is upstream spinning where the quill minnow is the bait *par excellence*. Small, fast-flowing upland country streams, with plenty of riffles and boulders and overhanging trees, are the ideal locations for this type of fishing. It requires a very similar approach to upstream worming.

When possible, the best way is actually to get into the river and work slowly upstream, casting directly up and in front into the likely places. Cover all the water and move forwards a few paces after each cast, searching holes under the banks and behind tree roots even if the water is quite shallow. It is essential to spin fast and to cast as far forwards as possible to cover fish that are completely unaware of your presence. This is, of course, an excellent way of catching brown trout and many will be caught. The larger ones that can be kept are a bonus, but the smaller fish can be a menace for to catch one may disturb a particularly good spot and the small trout and parr that shoot ahead out of the shallows will transmit their panic to the rest of the pool, making it a useless location. The art of upstream spinning is not quickly learned, because it provides the most difficult of

casting situations in avoiding overhanging trees and bushes to reach the
productive areas. Almost every cast requires a different skill or technique
for direction and distance.

Tackle

The fixed-spool reel The fixed-spool reel, sometimes called the open-
face reel, is now the universal instrument for spinning. It has had an odd
history of development and acceptance by anglers has been a slow process.
The forerunners of the modern type were crude by modern standards but
reasonably efficient. It was the 'Illingworth' that started it all. This model,
together with the 'Allcock Stanley' which came on the market in 1934, is
probably the best known of the prototypes. These reels had a manual
pick-up which required quite considerable dexterity to operate and
numerous spinners must have been lost on the bottom in shallow water.
Many different mechanical ideas were tried out. On the early 'Stanley'
reels it was the pick-up that moved in and out to spread the line evenly
over the spool and not the spool itself. Other inventive ideas appeared with
the 'Felton Crosswind', which had the spool offset at an angle so that each
wind overlapped the previous one, and the casting reel made by 'Alvey'
that had a drum which could be turned through 90° and so could be used
as a centre pin or a fixed-spool. Hardy's came on the scene with the 'Altex',
a reel so well made and reliable that some are still seen in use today.

By 1950, fixed-spool reels were generally available from all tackle
dealers, but for some reason the French manufacturers seemed to have
taken over and most of the better, cheaper reels around that time were of
French, or continental, origin. Some would say that the French still lead
the field. Through the 'fifties the most popular British reel was probably
the 'Ambidex', a reel noted for its dependability.

Why did such a useful tool take so many years to find its way into every
angler's tackle armoury? Much of the blame must lie with Alex Wanless,
an experienced, clever and notable angler in his day. In 1932 he coined the
phrase 'thread line spinning', and for the next twenty years the fixed-spool
reel was never to realise its full potential.

A fixed-spool reel was to be used, he said, for thread line spinning, since
that was the only sporting way of using such an instrument. Certain rules
were laid down as to the breaking strength of lines allowed. These were not
more than 2 lb for brown trout (you could go up to 4 lb if fishing where
large brown trout could be expected), not more than 4 lb for sea trout and
not more than 6 lb for salmon. Line strengths were coupled to rod lengths
and test curves, and so on, to make up complete thread-lining outfits.
Hardy's even started making special devon minnows for thread-lining that
were small and made of lead and other heavy alloys. It was claimed, and
rightly so, that huge distances, never before conceived, could be cast with
this equipment. What that had to do with their practical use for angling
seemed immaterial. Incredibly, Wanless wrote, 'Observance of these standards will put the beginner on the right road'.

Because casting had become so easy with a fixed-spool reel and far more water could now be fished at a faster rate, it was considered unsporting and the thread-lining principle was accepted as the only fair method of using such a reel. The theory behind it all was that with the slipping clutch set correctly line breakage was impossible, for any jerks or pulls while playing a fish would simply draw line from the reel. There were even those who advocated pointing the rod tip straight at a hooked fish wherever it went and playing it solely on the reel. Amazing feats by anglers were reported

Use of the fixed spool reel

in the press and a record salmon of 54 lb on 6 lb line was claimed from a Norwegian river. Nothing was said of the multitude of fish breaking free with yards of line attached. The spinner trade at the time must have been booming.

In 1951 and 1952 angling writers began to suggest that, far from being sporting, thread-lining was just the opposite. Such a high proportion of fish were being lost on light lines that the strengths began to creep up to a more realistic 8 or 10 lb, and by 1955 the method had died a befitting death and much more sensible lines of 10 lb for sea trout and 15 lb or so for salmon were being used. Manufacture and sale of fixed-spool reels took off and they became the accepted tool that they are today. It is very uncommon these days, but nevertheless quite a joy, to see a sea trout or salmon angler spinning with a centre-pin reel.

Once a beginner learns to cast with a fixed-spool reel the action becomes smooth and simple, provided one or two basic rules are observed. Assuming the angler is right-handed, then the left hand lifts the bale arm and winds the reel, nothing else. The right hand holds the rod and the index finger on this hand holds the line prior to casting. It is best to forget all about the overhead method of tournament casting—it has no place in sea trout fishing. The method is usually associated with the multiplier, a form of free-running centre-pin reel which is useful for some types of fishing but not sea trout.

There are a few points to look for in a good, dependable fixed-spool reel. It should have a fibre or brush skirt around the base of the spool to prevent the line catching under it, a common fault with early types. The bale arm fitted with a static, toughened line guide rather than a roller bearing is better. The line can get caught between the roller and the bale arm of the latter if the screw works loose, and is the cause of many a lost fish. Any screw or working part can come loose, so the reel should be checked carefully before beginning to fish and at intervals thereafter. A reel is a piece of machinery and, like a car, there has not been one invented that will not let you down at one time or another. If travelling some distance from base carry a spare, the time will come when it will be sorely needed. There is nothing more annoying than walking three miles and at the third or fourth cast losing a screw from the handle or suffering some other mechanical mishap. It happened to me once many years ago and it will never happen again. There is now a variety of gearings available on modern reels and the high retrieve rate of some can be most useful in methods like upstream spinning in clear water.

Lines The development of lines for spinning was perhaps linked in some way to the slow increase in popularity of the fixed-spool reel, nylon monofilament only being generally available and accepted when this reel became widely used. A synthetic line call 'Jagut' (from Japanese gut) was available from Allcock's as early as 1918 and was still being offered in their catalogue of 1936. The change from natural gut to nylon, called gut substitute in the early days, was opposed in the main by anglers. When nylon line became available the old gut was still regarded as much more reliable, especially for casts and leaders. As late as 1950 Hardy's catalogue listed thirteen different types of gut casts to only one of nylon and only one make of spooled nylon was offered—'Luxor' (inevitably made in France). Nylon was described as having a shorter life than gut, was not so dependable and was very liable to slip when knotted. Silk or synthetic braided line were the popular choices for spinning for many years, but around the mid-'fifties, almost overnight, nylon was accepted as the only really ideal line to marry with a fixed-spool reel and attained its rightful place.

Today nylon lines are so well made that there is little advice one can give as to choice. I prefer a line that is supple, does not flash in the light and is dull, watery grey or green in colour.

The major line trouble when spinning is from fraying, sometimes caused by a fault on the reel but more often by a faulty rod ring, especially the tip. If the agatine centre of a rod ring falls out, the line can be quickly ruined. The problem also occurs when a tip ring has become grooved from much use. Line kinking is not the fault of the line or the reel: it is the angler's fault for not using enough, or efficient, swivels.

Nylon line does deteriorate over a period of time, especially if exposed to bright light, as it must be from time to time, and so it should be changed or turned end for end after a season's use. I buy good quality, but cheaper, bulk spools for spinning line and change any suspect line on the reel as soon as possible. Needless to say, if this is done in the car park or on the river bank the old nylon should be taken home and burned, not discarded.

Spinning line for sea trout can vary according to the conditions; 6 lb or at the most 8 lb is what is required for upstream, clear water work, while 10 or 12 is ideal for coloured, heavy water. In larger rivers when spinning, particularly in heavy water, there is always the likelihood of hooking a salmon, so the line chosen should suit the occasion. The strength of line will depend to a certain degree on the choice of lure. For instance, a number one mepps will not marry with 15 lb line and neither will the largest size toby be much use at the end of a 6 lb line.

Casts I like to use casts of 2 or 3 lb less breaking strain than the main line. This means that, together with less knot strength at the bait end, there will only be a short length lost on the occasional inevitable hang-up, with no decrease in the length of the main line. The result of not complying with this wise rule is shown when catching someone else's line while fishing and, on winding in some thirty yards over the fingers, it is found that some previous angler was stuck on the bottom of the pool above.

When spinning a devon, a minimum of three swivels is required (as a rule one is incorporated in the mount) and any other form of bait needs at least two if line twisting is to be avoided. Line kinking does not only produce tangles and inconvenience, it is also often the cause of lost fish. Distance between swivels should be about eighteen inches and no swivel should be more than about four feet from the bait. This means that the line can be wound in sufficiently to allow a comfortable casting swing without having to wind a swivel into the tip ring. Swivels should not be cast through the rod rings otherwise the rings will be damaged and will fray the line.

Hooks Close attention should be given to hooks at all times, for they are, without doubt, the most important item of tackle. That is not to say they are the best looked after; often they are sadly overlooked or considered to be worthy of only minor attention. Hooks on spinning baits require the most attention of all, for it is these that are subject to most abuse. It is surprising how many anglers keep on fishing right through numerous snags on the bottom or after hang-ups in trees. Each time the lure comes into contact with something, even a fish, it should be examined, a process that only takes just a couple of seconds, to make sure that nothing is amiss. A quick scan will reveal if the treble has been pulled out of line or a hook straightened or broken. Spinning can result most frustratingly in many runs without a fish being hooked and there is no doubt that often it is the hooks that are at fault.

Some hooks, even when new, are simply not sharp enough. Stubby points very quickly become blunted and give poor penetration. The point should be reasonably long and quite sharp. The barb should be neither too big nor too small, and special attention should be given to whether it has been cut too deep, thereby weakening the point. Forget barbless hooks for sea trout, no matter how sportsmanlike you wish to be.

I carry a small sharpening stone with me all the time when spinning and lightly hone each point to a fine sharpness before starting to fish; I then sharpen up as necessary thereafter. If fishing with a heavy bait, occasionally bumping the bottom, this has to be done fairly frequently. One drawback is that the constant honing wears down the points to the stage at which they become stubby and short, and when this happens it is time to change to a fresh treble. I may change the treble on a favourite spinner two or three times in a day's fishing. It may seem a lot, but I lose few fish once hooked. Hooks, even treble hooks, expensive as they are, are a small price to pay for success.

My advice would be: if in doubt about the effectiveness of a hook it should be discarded. Like line, hooks should be disposed of at home. Cattle or sheep can pick them up in their hooves and the loss of an animal (and your fishing) could result.

Rods I have little to say about spinning rods for sea trout. There is plenty of choice and each individual should fish a rod that feels right for him. A two-piece, hollow fibreglass 8 feet rod should be suitable for most people. If carbon fibre is your choice and fishing with a delicate wand is preferred, so be it. Personally, I find most of them hopelessly out of balance once the reel has been fitted.

Hooking, Playing and Landing

The thump of a good sea trout as it seizes the spinner is one of the highlights of the sport. Takes can vary from a very hard tug to an almost imperceptible change in the progress of the lure. When a fish takes food it

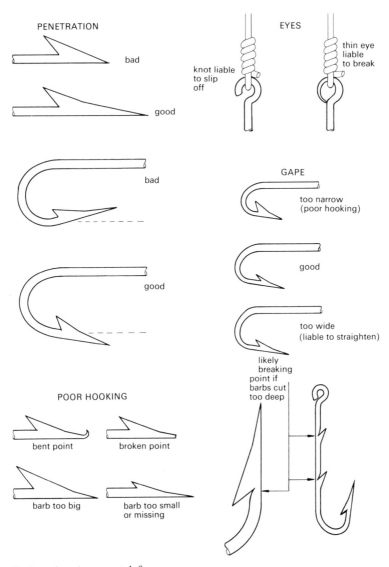

Hooks—the points to watch for

seizes it in its mouth and almost invariably follows this with a firm, sharp shake of its head from side to side. This is to aid swallowing, for it has to move the food into position in its mouth in that way because the tongue is fixed, not flexible. The bite that is felt when a fish takes a worm varies from a series of taps from a small fish to several firm pulls from a large one, and is caused by the side to side head movement. If a fish takes hold of a spinner and the first head movement is *away* from the angler, then this is the classic, thrilling 'smash-take'. If the first tug is *towards* the angler, the run is far less dramatic. Sometimes a fish will seize a spinner from directly behind and keep on swimming towards the angler. This is the type of run where hardly a pull is felt at all, merely a feeling that something has interrupted the spinner's progress. The catching of a leaf can give a similar effect. Hooking the 'bottom' is another fairly common sort of run when a fish finds a spinner crossing its path and simply opens its mouth to take it. The side-swallow movement does not take place, as the fish is caught unawares and does not move until the angler strikes or it feels the hooks bite home. On very rare occasions the static take goes on for several seconds, but the pause is often of far less duration than the angler realises before the action starts.

Striking Whether to strike while spinning is a question that is regularly asked. It is a difficult one to answer because each type of run really needs a different approach. The smash-take obviously does not require a strike, for the fish will already have hooked itself if it is going to at all. The light follow-up take, on the other hand, definitely does require one to drive the hooks in, otherwise the fish will open its mouth when it realises that the bait is not eatable and the spinner will, in most cases, come free. There is no way that an angler, no matter how experienced he is or how quick his reflexes, is going to decide in a split second whether to strike according to the run. The best policy is to strike every time to make sure. I like to make a firm, sharp strike within the limitations of the line being used.

Much depends on the angler's preference as regards the slipping clutch and how much tension to set. If fishing light lines on the thread-line principle, then there is little point in striking for the clutch will merely slip. Many fish are lost through poor hooking as well as breakage when using this technique. When using heavier lines of 12 to 14lb the clutch can be set to enable a good strike to be made and at the same time eliminate a possible break. The unorthodox method, which I use, is to have the clutch on tight so that no line will give at all. I find that this is the best for good hooking. There is always some give in nylon monofilament and this, coupled with the spring of the rod, gives enough of a buffer action for the very hard take; I have rarely lost a fish in such a way because of line breakage. When a fish has been lost due to a break, it has nearly always been traced to a bad swivel, poorly-tied knot or other fault such as an unnoticed frayed line. It only takes a second to release tension on the clutch after a fish is hooked, if so desired. Even when salmon fishing I always have the clutch on solid and play the fish on the reel. The backreeling technique to a fast running fish is not always recommended to the faint hearted or the inexperienced, especially when the reel handle is pulled through the fingers at high speed, but I have never lost a fish because of it—though I must admit to the danger of such a practice. That is the way I prefer to do it and it is the best way to keep in constant touch with fish. A fish racing downstream dragging line from a poorly adjusted clutch with little resistance is a lost cause. It goes without saying that with the clutch-tight method, the reverse gear must be open to allow back pedalling where necessary. At the other extreme is the angler who has the clutch set so loose that the fish can do just as it likes and, if it is not lost, usually takes ten times longer to land than it should.

Playing Once a fish is hooked, playing it on a fixed-spool outfit is fairly straightforward and much more control is possible on the fish's movements than with a centre pin reel. With the latter a fish charging towards the angler can cause some hairy moments, but a fixed-spool, with its higher gearing, enables contact to be maintained. With experience, an angler can sense whether a fish is well hooked or not. Generally, one that fights on the surface and leaps from the water is not a well-hooked fish, while a fish that bores and stays deep, is. This is not, however, a hard and fast rule.

There is one very common form of behaviour peculiar to freshly hooked sea trout that is difficult to deal with and very often results in a lost fish. This is tumbling. Tumbling occurs when a fish takes the lure close to the surface in fast flowing water and is caused by the fish's vigorous swimming motions in trying to escape. The arch of the body is thrust from side to side, which would normally result in a burst of forward speed. However, because the fish is so near the surface, or on it, there is not enough water resistance to get a bite and the result is a rapid and exaggerated flapping from side to side, which looks just as if the fish is tumbling over end to end.

A tumbling fish that is only lightly hooked will almost certainly throw the spinner. If the line is slackened off to allow the fish to submerge, the movements will stop but the hook hold may also be released and at the point of slackening the fish's tail may slap the line, thereby pulling the hook out. If strain is tightened, this will encourage the fish to tumble more vigorously until it is exhausted. It is certainly the quickest but most dangerous way of playing a fish out. The only effective, evasive action possible is to lower the rod tip to water level at the side in the same way that side strain is applied. This lowers the direction of pull and should encourage the fish to move off the surface, when tumbling will stop.

The best method of landing sea trout on a spinner, whenever possible, is to beach them. The only other real alternative is a landing net; gaffs and tailers are not suitable. Great care must be taken with a landing net when fishing with a multi-hooked lure to ensure that the netting does not catch in loose hooks.

Otherwise normal rules apply as regards net in the water and fish in head-first. With the stronger rod and line, as opposed to fly tackle, smaller fish can be lifted from the water where the bank is high and the waterside inaccessible. This method should only be a last resort, however, and is not to be recommended. A fish should be completely played out and have ceased struggling before such action is attempted.

Snag Release

This section on spinning would not be complete without some advice on how to release baits caught up on the river bottom or in trees. Spinners and lures are so expensive these days that it is always worth trying every possible method of release to reduce the number of losses which will happen from time to time. The difficult cast under the trees or the slow retrieve to draw near to the bottom always carry the risk, no matter how experienced the angler happens to be.

When caught up on the bottom it is likely that one of three things has happened. The treble may have caught on a stone or ledge of rock, become wedged between stones or rocks, or worse still, been fouled by an underwater obstruction, the most common of which are sunken logs or tree branches.

In the first instance the lure will probably come free quite easily once slack line is given out. In the second, some specialised ploys may be required and the third, with one possible exception, is a hopeless case.

If a spinner fouls the bottom and refuses to come free, the obvious answer to the problem is to impart strain in the opposite direction to that in which it was travelling when it became caught. If spinning upstream at the time, all that is usually needed is a short walk downstream and a pull in the opposite direction. If a pull from the opposite bank is required, then a friendly angler on the other side may help by casting over your line and pulling from his side. If the river is shallow enough to cross it can be done by yourself. A stubbornly hung-up bait may sometimes be released by the use of an improvised otter. Specially made otters that slip over the line can be purchased at tackle shops, but a forked stick with one leg twice as long as the other will do the job just as well. Get out in the river as near as possible to directly upstream of the snag, hook the stick over the line and allow it to slide down, at the same time paying out slack. The otter will run down to a point below the bait and should pull it free downstream. If not, a sharp tug on the line will usually do the trick.

If the bait still refuses to shift, then it is more likely that the snag is a sunken log or branch. The only way that the hook can be persuaded to come away is by imparting a steady pull on the line to see if the obstruction will pull free or break away. Sunken timber is often very rotten and will break under strain. The only way that a hook will pull out of fresh wood is if it straightens before the line breaks.

Another common problem is when, having cast too far, the bait lands in the bushes on the far bank. If the spinner is seen to wind itself around a branch, then it is lost unless it can be reached and disentangled by hand. A simple trick with a spinner that has been cast into the bushes is to give it a sudden, sharp snatch. This very often results in the bait flying back through the twigs and leaves instead of becoming irretrievably fast.

A word of warning in conclusion. When pulling a bait from a tree, always turn away from the scene of action. A spinner coming free all at once on a stretched nylon line travels like a bullet.

9

Worm Fishing

Fishing with a worm for sea trout or salmon has become associated with a certain amount of stigma and not a little criticism from some anglers and angling writers. Authors have written phrases such as 'the abhorrent practice of worming', 'in the event of a flood the wormers appear like leeches' or 'a practice of a less sporting nature could not be imagined'. These extremes of view are hard to understand, particularly since many such authors have not even sampled the method. To the sea trout beginner, who to gain knowledge before starting reads the many and varied books on the subject of angling, the damning of the worm as a bait can be most misleading.

I know of an angler who fly fished the Teifi for salmon for over ten years and who went to his grave without ever catching a single fish. No doubt he enjoyed his angling to a certain extent but refusal to try any other method must have resulted in frustration beyond all reason. Why then has the worm, or 'bait' fishing as it is sometimes known, been given such an antisocial place in the game fishing world? Coarse fishermen are quite happy to use the worm or maggot without fear of condemnation and their policy is to return fish unharmed to the water, a practice considered to be the ultimate display of sportsmanship in sea trout or salmon angling. Is game fishing more sporting than coarse fishing? Many would say it is not.

The reasons for condemnation of worming are variously given as:

1. It disturbs the water and the fish.
2. It is too deadly.
3. The fish gorge the bait.
4. It is unsporting.
5. It is the least exciting method.
6. It requires no skill.

To put these points into perspective let us look at them in a little more detail and see if there is any basis of truth in them.

1. Bait fishing is probably the least disturbing of angling methods, for far less casting takes place and the angler remains stationary for longer periods, often merely sitting on the river bank. This makes him much less conspicuous than a man spinning or fly fishing who is, of necessity, moving about and even waving his arms as casting takes place. To be controversial, I would say that an angler working a pool with a fourteen feet fly rod, a line

of near rope-like proportions and a three inch tube is disturbing the water and the fish far more than any worm fisherman ever could.

2. There is no doubt that under certain water conditions, and in the right hands, worming can be a very effective method of catching fish. No more so, however, than other methods when the conditions are favourable.

3. When in the majority of cases the fish that is to be caught is to be killed, it seems of little consequence that it should swallow the hook. Coarse fishermen, who frequently use a worm, return all their fish alive to the water. If a sea trout that has gorged a worm is to be given its freedom, the nylon cast can be cut and the fish freed without even the need to handle it. The price of a hook is little to pay for the sport obtained and the fish's natural body juices will soon dissolve the metal. Few fish die from having hooks buried in them, provided they are not played to the point of exhaustion.

4. The unsporting tag is attached because of a misguided opinion that worming is in some way unfair. It is a legitimate form of angling unless banned by byelaw or club rule and, therefore, is a fair method should the angler wish to use it.

5. There are those anglers (and I include myself among them) who would consider that the ultimate angling experience, and a sure fire adrenalin producer, is to have a salmon or large sea trout seize a worm being trotted down the centre of a pool. A fly fisherman would argue that the rise of a good fish is a similarly delightful experience. Many anglers who employ both methods, however, would say that worming and fly fishing take ranks equally, or that worming has even better excitement value. Numerous worm fishermen are fly fishermen as well, but there is a band of fly-only stalwarts who never fish with a worm for reasons already explained.

6. There are a multitude of ways of fishing with a worm. The general concept to the uninitiated is of an angler sitting by the river with a lump of lead holding a static, lifeless worm on the bottom. This must be, admittedly, one of the least rewarding types of angling but, nevertheless, does produce fish on occasions. Those who sit for hours fishing in such a fashion, 'hogging' one spot and so preventing others from fishing, are beyond what it is possible to put in print. It is not only worm fishermen that do this—some fly fishermen are equally to blame. The art of worming as practised by a skilful angler is the most difficult and exciting sport of all, and can produce rich rewards.

In a Flood

There are times when sea trout enter the smaller rivers from the sea in shoals and this is usually during summer floods. After a deep depression has passed over or a thunderstorm has released its deluge the rivers swell and rise, sometimes a couple of feet or more. The water becomes thick and brown, and large amounts of debris, leaves and branches wash down to the sea. This multifold increase in fresh water entering the sea spreads outwards and attracts the sea trout to the river. The fish know that this is the time when they can get into the river easily and travel upstream to the deeper holding pools in safety. A flood may occur several times in the period from June to September when sea trout run, or only once or twice; in some years sufficient rain never falls and the sea trout need to creep in at night with backs out of the water on the shallow or else wait for the autumn rains later in the year. However, after a flood occurs there are many sea trout anglers who have been waiting for such an event and who now gather on the river banks. The sea trout run is on.

Sea trout entering fresh water from the sea undergo a dramatic physical change to adapt to osmotic pressure. Their sense and alertness are nullified by their preoccupation with bodily functions and, as a consequence, they are more easily tempted by anglers. In rivers with large estuaries, where salt to fresh water changes gradually, their journey is relatively easy, but in smaller rivers, like short Welsh or Scottish mountain torrents that empty directly into the sea, it is much more difficult.

Because they are easier to catch, some would frown upon anglers who fish at this time. An authority on game angling in his time wrote in 1936, 'The man who catches trout in coloured water on worm or gentle is greatly to be pitied'. He was writing an article giving advice to beginners, would you believe? The gentle (maggot) has long since disappeared from the game angling scene, but I wonder how many newcomers to the sport have savoured their first thrills of angling, young and old alike, while worming in a flood and then progressed onwards to the angling specialisation of their choice. Flood worming is so short-lived and perhaps only happens about twice in a season, so why not take advantage when it does? Sometimes to the old and infirm it is a godsend. Many years ago, before large tracts of bog and marshland were drained by Water Authority engineers, even a summer flood would last a couple of days, but now a few hours of heavy water is all that can be expected. In any case, at this time of year dry land, evaporation and plant growth cause rivers to run off very quickly to their former levels.

There are many who take advantage of these conditions and simply sit on a stool on the bank and allow the worm to rest on the bottom until a fish takes it, as fish will from time to time. The more skilful angler will 'read' the water and pick out likely spots where fish may be resting on their journey upstream. At this stage the sea trout will be right in towards the bank, just off the grass if the flood water is heavy. A quietly flowing eddy at the side of the main stream, such as is found on the inside of a bend or behind a boulder or projection on the bank, is the spot to look for.

Examining the River A place where the flow is still directed downstream, but much less powerful than the main current, is ideal, rather than a still area or a back-flowing eddy. To be able to extract full value from this type of fishing, an examination of the river when the flows are low and clear can be of immense value in detecting possible lies during flood conditions. A large stone near the bank which may be used as a fishing platform when the river is low can create an ideal lie in heavy flows. When submerged the obstruction causes a slowing of the current both above and below and fish will use these areas as resting places away from the main current. In dirty flood water quite large fish will rest in depths of no more than about eighteen inches.

Using a light lead some twelve inches above the hook, with a single red worm, cover the water by continually trotting down the current. Just enough weight to hold the bottom, usually only one or two split shot, is sufficient. Each time the weight holds bottom leave it for thirty seconds or so, making sure that it is not a fish that has interrupted its progress, then gently lift it free and allow the worm to drop further downstream. In this way far more water will be covered than with a static bait approach. In these conditions it is probably the only time that an angler has to get the bait right to the fish instead of the fish coming to the bait. After trotting down at different distances from the bank, remembering of course that fish may be lying right at your feet, and having covered all likely lies it is best to move on to another spot. In some cases, as when fish can be seen travelling, different fish may be continually moving through and it may pay to remain in the same place for longer than it takes to cover all the likely water. Travelling sea trout often show by porpoising at the surface in a similar fashion to travelling salmon. If fishing close to a weir or obstruction sea trout will, of course, be seen jumping or swimming with a 'whoosh' through the fast water.

The tough red worms that are found in rotting vegetation and compost heaps are the only ones that really work well in this sort of fishing. Other types are much less effective and, indeed, the grey lobs are often useless. Some flood wormers lay out newspaper and hessian sacks on the garden to attract the red worms. The next best thing is a newly rotting compost heap, but to encourage them to breed it must be kept very damp.

The Catch It must be said that the main catch under these conditions will be whitling from 10 oz to 1 lb in weight, probably fish straight from the sea with lice covering the nose and back. The occasional larger fish will be hooked and that can be something of a problem at times. If the fish behaves and the angler is skilful enough to keep it close and out of the current, then all will be well, but a heavy fish that charges downstream, as some tend to do in heavy coloured water, is very likely to be lost. Even in very dirty water it is not wise to use tackle that is too heavy, since the fish may be shy of seizing the worm. A hook size 6 on 8 lb nylon is just about right. Some would prefer stouter tackle for, if fishing in a river that also contains salmon, one may be encountered and a difficult proposition it may turn out to be. The larger brethren do not take a worm so freely in heavy flood water, however, and though I have taken many salmon in near flood conditions on a worm I have only once caught one on a small red worm meant for sea trout. For the best hooking potential, short shank, wide gape hooks are needed. A single worm threaded from the head or the mantle around the bend to bury the hook completely is the method. None of your loosely-hooked worms here, like the lightly-nicked lob for chub.

Sea trout are very wise fish and the hook needs to be completely covered, even the eye. It is also essential to fish with a fresh offering. They will not be interested in a pale, limp, drowned and lifeless worm, or even one that has been marked by the needle sharp teeth of small trout or has had its tail nipped off. Change it frequently.

The knock of a sea trout is a distinct tap at short intervals and can soon be distinguished from the nibble of small trout or parr which will be a nuisance on occasions. It is better to pull the worm away from the smaller fish to prevent their swallowing the bait completely, causing both injury and possible death to what should always be regarded as future recruits.

Sometimes a sea trout will feel the hook and move off, while at other times it will remain quite stationary with the bait in its mouth. The experienced angler will know instinctively whether it is the bottom or a fish. When a fish is felt, it is best to wait for several seconds to allow the bait to be taken into its mouth and then a short, sharp strike is necessary, with the rod inclined downstream to drive the hook home. The practice carried out by some flood wormers of laying the rod down when a bite is felt and lighting up a cigarette or otherwise killing time so that the fish will gorge the bait is to be condemned most strongly. Such a method is certainly unsporting and totally unnecessary. The strike usually pulls the hook into the corner of the jaw, which gives a firm hook hold.

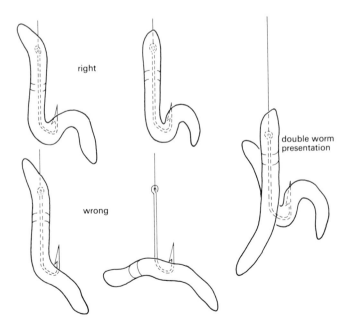

Hooking a worm

If when fishing there is little or no activity, it pays to be a little patient for the river may still be rising. Sea trout will travel at this time but for some reason are usually reluctant to take a bait. As soon as the water reaches its peak and starts to fall sport should improve.

There are times when the whitling shoals are in the river that many fish are caught by this method. Half a dozen of these beautiful fighting creatures should be enough to please any angler and cause him to be satisfied for that day. Some angling clubs have sensible rules, like the one of the Aberaeron Town Angling Club which limits the amount of sea trout allowed to ten in any one day.

Tackle in a flood For flood worming a fairly stout rod of eight or nine feet in length is required. As distance casting is not involved, a centre-pin is just as useful as a fixed-spool reel, unless the river is large. An ideal rod for this type of fishing cannot be bought and has to be made up by the angler himself or a rod-making friend. A spinning-rod blank is employed, with the reel fitting at the butt like a fly rod. A fairly stiff hollow fibre glass blank of nine feet, made up with a centre-pin reel at the butt, is a nicely balanced rod and can be held comfortably for long periods. The angler who holds his rod while worming and works the lies will do considerably better, as a rule, than the one with the lazy, forked-stick approach.

The reel's main line should be strong, around 15 to 20 lb, not that great strength is needed but on a centre-pin thick line is much easier to control. A yard or so of attached cast, of from 4 to 10 lb, is all that is required at the action end. Cast rigs will vary according to individual taste, but one of the best is a small swivel tied to the end of the main line and the necessary shot or running lead fixed to the main line with the swivel acting as a stopper. The hook is then tied to a lighter cast of about eighteen inches. This means

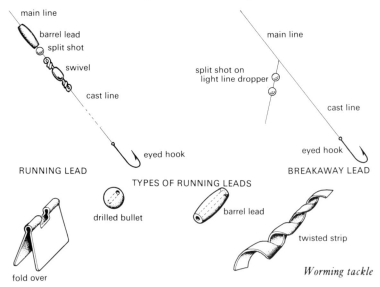

Worming tackle

that if the hook becomes caught on a snag, the lighter cast will break first
and only the hook will be lost. Should the lead catch, the stronger main line
will usually allow it to be pulled free. Another rig sometimes favoured is to
have the leads on a lighter breaking-strain dropper, so that if the lead gets
fouled the dropper will break and the remainder can be retrieved. In such
fishing it is the lead that most commonly gets caught and this method can
result in annoyingly frequent lead changes.

In clear water Worming in clear water is a quite different technique
from heavy water fishing. It is much more difficult to tempt fish and in this
type of fishing concealment is as important as the actual fishing method.
In clear water the approach should always be made in an upstream direction. Fish lie with their heads pointing upstream into the current and,
therefore, they are easily able to detect anglers approaching towards them.
When walking upstream, if possible stand at water level below the bank-
line. If it is necessary to walk along the bank, a background of trees or
rising land will help concealment. It is very easy for fish to detect moving
objects against the skyline, sometimes at quite a distance. Clothing needs
to be of a sombre hue—browns or greens—and you should avoid anything
bright or light in colour which can easily be seen by the fish. It is odd how
some anglers insist on wearing white or yellow garments, which although
not quite so bad when the water is coloured are sporting suicide when it
is clear. I recall an angler on a fortnight's holiday at one of the local hotels
on the Teifi, who wore a white pullover all the time he was fishing. He
complained bitterly that though other anglers were catching fish, he could
catch nothing. These other anglers (including myself) were just too polite
to point out to him his ridiculous clothing, but simply dubbed him 'Mr
Persil' and kept well away.

Upstream worming requires the lightest tackle of all sea trout fishing.
About 4 lb to a number 8 hook is the preferred rig, with just enough shot
to provide weight for casting out. If it is possible to cast out with only the
weight of the worm, then all the better for as natural a presentation as
possible is required. Always keep down out of sight and cast as far upstream into the deeper pools and riffles as the limits of the tackle and
overhanging branches will allow. Holes under overhanging tree stumps
and in the shelter of boulders are the sort of places that sea trout inhabit
in low water. Let the worm trot downstream naturally, retrieving line as
it does to keep in contact all the time. It is necessary to be as still as
possible, for sometimes a fish will follow the worm some distance downstream and take it in full view. If there is plenty of background cover of
trees and bushes, it may not suspect that there is anything amiss until the
hook is gently but firmly driven home. Polaroid sunglasses can be a useful
addition to the equipment.

Compost red worms are the best but if it is possible to get some brandlings or manure worms they will do almost equally as well. Smaller and
softer than the red worms, they do not stay on the hook so well but sea
trout love their succulence.

If fishing in small pools, it is of little use continuing in that spot after catching a fish for the disturbance will have put off the other inhabitants, at least for that day. In larger rivers it may be worth continuing in a successful place for a while longer, because in deeper water there is less disturbance and other fish may come to the bait. This type of fishing is best carried out in the remoter parts of the river where there has been less disturbance from anglers—unfortunately not very often possible these days, especially on club or association waters. Nevertheless, it is always worth seeking out the more remote areas of river away from the crowds, perhaps where there are no access roads or places which are inaccessible because of trees or undergrowth. Upstream worming can pay dividends in the lonelier, undisturbed reaches of the river, bearing in mind that sea trout, particularly late in the season, may have travelled well up into such areas.

It must be said that this method is also very good for brown trout and, even if no sea trout are caught, there could still be the bonus of a decent bag of brownies on the day.

Another method of clear water bait fishing is drop-minnow, or dip-and-draw as it is sometimes called. It is popular in some parts of Wales, particularly Carmarthenshire and in a few areas of mid-Wales. It certainly cannot be classed as spinning, so perhaps it would be appropriate to mention it here. Oddly enough, this is about the only method of fishing that is effective in bright, sunny, low water conditions; in fact, some would say the brighter the sun and the lower and clearer the water, the better. It is an excellent method of taking brown trout and at times very effective for sea trout also, especially the smaller ones. There is a lot of preparation involved and that is probably the reason why the method has never been very popular. However, the actual preparation can be quite good fun and the rewards can be well worthwhile.

Minnows are collected alive, by using either a minute hook with a tiny piece of worm or a minnow trap. They are then transported in a bucket or jar and kept alive until required. A straight shank number 6 hook, whipped to light monofilament, is used with a drilled torpedo lead. The lead lies on the shank of the hook and the whole is threaded with a needle through the fish from the mouth to the tail. The hook bend is pulled into the side of the mouth where it is least conspicuous.

A long rod is used, about a twelve-feet salmon fly rod being the favourite tool. This enables the angler to lower the minnow in between weed beds or into holes under the bank or behind stones, while at the same time remaining well back out of sight. The minnow is allowed to sink, spiralling downwards, and is then lifted and allowed to sink once more. The method can be varied and small tweaks of the bait to imitate a sick or injured fish can prove irresistible. A bite is usually a sudden and savage series of jerks as the fish seizes the bait and turns for its hideaway. Line must be given immediately and the fish given time to turn the minnow into its mouth head first, after which a light strike should produce a sea trout. As in all clear water fishing, keeping out of sight is of paramount importance.

Tackle in clear water There are two completely different outfits that can be employed in clear water worming. The first is a fly rod rigged as for fly fishing, with a floating line and, instead of a fly at the end of the cast, a small hook on to which is threaded a little red worm. No weight is needed. The whole is cast out deftly in the same manner as a fly—casting upstream and retrieving with the current. It is necessary to strike at a bite almost instantly or the fish will very quickly feel the drag at the line as it pulls downstream. This is a delightfully skilled method and demands considerable dexterity on the part of the angler. There are, however, one or two distinct disadvantages to this approach. Casting distance is somewhat restricted and the bait can easily be cast off the hook. Overhanging trees can prevent lies being covered and can even prevent some stretches of river from being fished at all. Most importantly, though, it does involve a certain amount of movement in casting which in clear, low water can frighten the quarry unless great efforts are made towards concealment.

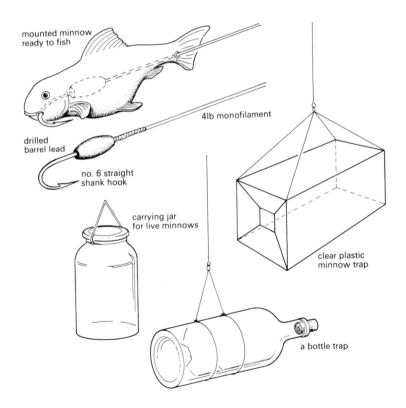

Drop minnow tackle

The second method is the use of a fixed-spool reel and a light spinning rod. If the reel spool is loaded with light 4 or 6 lb monofilament and the rod is only 6 or 7 feet in length, some of the most inaccessible places can be reached. With experience, the worm can be dropped into likely holes under bushes and boulders at an appreciable distance where there is no likelihood of the fish detecting the angler's presence. If fishing with a very light line, there is rarely any need for weight except to get that little bit of extra casting distance or to sink the worm down into the deeper holes.

Whichever method is used, the emphasis must be on light lines and small hooks and baits. Needless to say, if a good-sized, fresh-run sea trout is hooked, it will have to be played very carefully on such light tackle. A landing net is essential and must be kept ready for instant use. A long-handled landing net over the shoulder may be not only quite useless but a danger to life and limb when you are crouched under the bank with only three feet of clearance between water surface and overhanging blackthorn, and a 4 lb sea trout forcibly expressing its desire for freedom. A small scoop net is the ideal instrument.

Tackle at night Common sense will dictate the type of tackle required for worming at night. Of necessity, simple tackle is wanted which will give the least trouble and the least likelihood of something going wrong. Fixed-spool reels are generally unsatisfactory. Clearing the line from behind the spool or a tangle around the bale arm, tasks which are rudimentary during the day, can become tedious and frustrating after dark. The best procedure is to stick to the tackle one is accustomed to. Lightness of tackle is not so important and neither is it necessary to be so particular about dress and movement. Providing the use of a torch is kept to a minimum, it is unlikely that the fish will be able to detect an angler's presence, providing he keeps away from high banks and other exposed places.

At this time it is probably more important than at any other to see to such comforts as warm underwear, dry boots and a hot flask with favourite contents, rather than the actual refinements of tackle.

At Night

Under no circumstances will a salmon take a worm at night. Not so the sea trout, however, and after dark fishing can be a fast and furious sport. The clearer the water the better, for they will not take well if the water is at all coloured and in flood water will not take a bait at all after dark. Of all the methods of sea trout fishing this is the one that I enjoy the least and rarely take part. It is usually necessary to keep still and remain in the same place for long periods. The fish are the ones that move around at night, not the fishermen. This results in an uncomfortable coldness creeping through the bones, for even in July and August it is quite surprising how cold it can get at night. On very dark nights fishing is done mostly by feel and instinct rather than sight, and casting in particular can be a very 'chuck it and chance it' affair. I personally would much rather fish with a fly, since there is greater control over line movement and positioning of the cast.

Nevertheless, there are those anglers who would class this sort of fishing among their favourites, and are sometimes very successful at it. Large fish are not so often encountered at night while worm fishing, which is perhaps just as well with the difficulties that large fish would present. Whitling are mostly caught, and on some nights they can become so easy to catch they virtually surrender themselves into the angler's bag. Needless to say, on others when the conditions seem to be perfect there will be no response whatsoever, but there lies the unpredictability which may be part of the attraction of the sport. Some anglers become experts at the art of trotting a small worm down through a pool in the darkness and these are usually the most successful. Others will be content with throwing the worm in and waiting for a fish to come along and find the bait. These latter 'sit-tight' types can be a real nuisance to fly fishermen who need more room and want to move about. For this reason several angling clubs do not allow night fishing with a worm on their water, or else restrict such activities to certain stretches of water only.

The same rules apply to shining a torch as apply to night fly fishing. If it is necessary to use a torch then the angler should move well away from the river bank or keep the light properly shaded. Regular night wormers are able to do all that is necessary, including threading a worm, without the benefit of a torch.

Later in the year, from about mid-July onwards, eels can be a nuisance. The maturing adults are beginning to move downstream from ponds and ditches on the first stage of their long trek to the breeding grounds in the Sargasso Sea, and will feed voraciously on their way down to the ocean. A large eel which has gorged the worm can be trouble beyond belief after dark, and the easiest solution is simply to cut it free and start again.

Night worm fishing can be productive throughout the dark hours, but by far the best times are the periods around dusk and the first hour or so after dark.

Types of Worm

There are several types of earthworm found in Britain which are suitable for sea trout fishing. Any of these species can be used to catch fish but some are much more successful than others.

The red worm, about three inches long when mature, is by far the best and most consistent catcher. This tough, hardy worm is found in compost or rotting vegetable matter and can quite easily be bred in the garden to give a constant supply. A compost heap covered in hessian sacks and kept damp during dry weather will provide their ideal habitat. It will help if the heap is in a cool corner of the garden close to a wall or under a tree and not subject to direct sunlight. Regular additions of household scraps, such as vegetable waste, potato peelings and the contents of the cold teapot as well as garden weeds, can all help production of the worm farm. These worms are fairly tough and easy to handle and, what is more important, they stay on the hook well and can withstand vigorous casting.

Brandlings are similar to red worms, but are smaller and softer. They like very damp conditions and can also be found in well rotted compost, but their favourite haunt is farmyard manure. They are not so popular for sea trout (though the fish like them well enough), because they are a little on the small side and two or three are needed on one hook to present a tempting mouthful. They do no stay on the hook as well and can be somewhat unpleasant to use for they secrete a yellow fluid which has an obnoxious smell.

The common lob worm, sometimes called the dew worm, is the largest British species and as such finds favour with salmon fishermen, for two or three on a large hook make an attractive bunch. They live best in cultivated, loamy soil. Being fairly soft they do not stay on the hook well and can break up when casting. They can be toughened up by leaving them to 'scour' in a container of moss for a few days. They are generally too large for sea trout, some specimens growing up to twelve inches in length, and although sometimes readily taken they are not nearly so effective as the red worms.

Collecting lob worms can be done when digging the garden, thereby carrying out two useful jobs at the same time. An easier method, though just as back breaking, is to collect them after dark when they emerge from their burrows on rainy nights. A good worming area can be spotted by the number of casts—small heaps of soil pushed up by burrowing worms. Well mown lawns, the vegetable garden, or even open fields are where they can be found. I recently discovered that mulched rose beds are particularly productive. It is a good idea to let neighbours know what is going on or there could be some embarrassing and amusing repercussions. I once had the police called out to investigate what some conscientious citizen thought was a suspicious character up to no good.

For collecting, two people are better than one: one to hold the torch and act as spotter, and the other to do the gathering. The worms are very quick to retreat down their holes and it is necessary to tread lightly. Use a fairly dim torch and do not shine it directly on to the worm. Once grasped, the worm should be drawn very carefully from the hole or it will break in two.

They can be kept for a considerable length of time in a plastic container, such as a dustbin with a tight fitting lid. Filled with equal quantities of moss and dead leaves, the whole should be kept damp and carefully examined every week or so. Any dead worms should be removed as they can affect the whole batch and much work will be wasted. It is essential to keep them cool and not allow the sun to shine directly on the bin. The corner of a cool shed or outhouse will do, but ideally the bin should be lowered into a hole in the garden which means that the worms, though captive, are able to live at their normal temperature.

When first gathered they are delicate and soft, but after a few days scouring in the leaf mould and moss they will become much tougher and lose most of their slimy covering.

The common earthworm, growing to about eight inches in length and found in compacted unproductive soils and sometimes in the garden while digging, is a poor bait and should only be used as a last resort.

10
Dealing with the Catch

Immediate Aftercare

It is a shame to see the way that some fish are treated after they have been killed. After providing exciting sport and an energetic fight for freedom, to be unceremoniously slung into the boot of a car or carried round for several hours till the skin dries out and colour drains away is no way to treat such a worthy quarry. If looked after properly to preserve its natural looks and condition, a fish is much more appreciated when it arrives in the kitchen, is given to friends, or, as is unfortunately sometimes the case, reaches the fishmonger's slab.

There are a few fortunate anglers who fish virtually on their doorsteps and I know of one who is able to fish from his back garden wall. Preservation of the catch is then unnecessary, for it can be on the table within the hour or placed immediately in the deep freeze for storage. However, if the angler is far from home then there are a number of ways to keep a fish in fresh condition for several hours or more.

The most effective method of keeping sea trout or salmon fresh is to place them in shallow wooden boxes and cover them with crushed ice as on commercial fishing boats. So stored, they will keep fresh for up to a week. I suppose it may be possible to find a wooden box at times somewhere along the river bank but never crushed ice, so other methods need to be employed.

Decomposition of flesh begins immediately on death and this process is greatly accelerated in the summer during warm weather. To keep a fish fresh it must be kept cool and to keep it cool it must be kept wet. At the same time it must have air circulating around it. A fish wrapped in a plastic bag in warm weather will deteriorate so rapidly as to render it unfit in only a few hours.

When carrying a fish on the bank it is best done with a finger through the gills or a piece of cord looped around its tail and passed through the gill arch. It can then be dipped in the river at frequent intervals to keep it fresh. An easy method of carrying is a landing net, but this can prove awkward if it is suddenly required for use on another hooked fish. Also, if left in the net for some time, the fish will stiffen and unsightly criss-cross patterns from the netting will mark it and spoil its appearance. When fishing some distance from home I carry a thin hessian sack in a coat pocket. This makes fish-carrying easy, especially if a shoulder laniard is affixed, for it can easily be dipped frequently in the water to keep the fish wet. To preserve a fish in tip-top condition it is always better to return to base, even if it may be half a mile away or more, rather than carry it around while continuing to fish. On return to fishing lodge or car, lay the fish flat in the wet sack with no other covering and keep it out of the sun. If it is a warm day and the car cannot be parked out of the sun under some trees or in the shade of a high bank, then the fish is best tucked away under the car in the shade. One problem with this practice, however, is the danger from hungry farmyard cats. An old fashioned idea to keep fish fresh was to wrap them in nettles but the reason for using this particular plant is obscure. Almost any foliage will do; ferns are ideal and far less cruel to the hands.

There is no need whatsoever to gut a sea trout when it is first caught: it will not deteriorate because of the presence of its entrails. The stomach will in all probability be empty and the gastric juices inoperative. This is not so if stockie-bashing on a reservoir has been the order of the day. In such a case it becomes almost essential to gut the caught trout as soon as possible, for the stomach contents of a fully-fed trout decompose far more quickly than the rest of the fish's flesh. The meat will become tainted in a very short time. It was once common practice to bleed freshly caught sea trout or salmon, but this is also totally unnecessary.

Cleaning and Dressing

With a little practice the gutting and cleaning of a sea trout is quite a simple operation. There are no messy stomach contents or evil smells to contend with. Strangely enough, the modern housewife's dislike of this simple task is probably the largest single drawback to the growth of the trout farming industry in Britain today, even though farmed fish are always starved before sale. It is essential to have a sharp knife for the job, a wooden carving board (the bread board will do) on a solid base, and either a bucket or plenty of old newspapers for the scraps. Some individuals keep all the bits and pieces and make a chowder—a kind of North American fish soup. Do not put them in the dustbin unless well wrapped in a plastic bag or the dustmen may be rightly peeved. It is also quite possible that rubbish will be found scattered all over the lawn when you reach for the milk in the morning, if marauding cats, a neighbour's dog, or even a cheeky fox scents the bin's internal delicacies.

The first stage of the cleaning process is to remove the scales. This is done by scraping the knife towards the head for, as the scales overlap rearwards, it means that the edge of the knife lifts the scales and pulls them out. Specially serrated knives for fish scaling can be purchased, but a good sharp kitchen knife will do just as well. It will be found that the fresher a fish (that is, fresh from the sea), the easier it is to scale. After some time in fresh water the skin becomes covered in a thick mucus and the scales are then much more difficult to remove.

Small fish can just be gutted, deheaded and the fins removed, or filleted. Larger fish can also be filleted, though this is only normally done prior to smoking. Usually they are gutted and cut into steaks or cutlets. To gut, cut a straight line from the point where the gill covers meet under the head, rearwards along the belly and between the paired pelvic fins to the vent. Grasp the entrails and pull them away. They are attached at the throat and a single cut here is all that is required to remove them. The kidney can then be seen lying under the backbone as a strip of dark, coagulated blood covered by a membrane. Slit the membrane along the whole of its length and scrape away the contents. A quick wash and the fish is ready for cooking. Smaller trout are traditionally cooked with the head and fins intact.

To fillet, first cut the head off. Then place the fish flat and, holding it firmly, cut the top fillet away by slicing just above the backbone, carefully and progressively parting flesh from bone. When the first fillet has been removed, turn the fish over and carry out the same procedure from the other side. With practice it is soon possible to take off two clean meaty fillets and discard the backbone with the fins still attached and the entrails encased. When cutting up a large fish, cut off the head first, then gut by slitting open the belly. Cut off all the fins and the tail. It may be necessary to tap the knife with a rolling pin or other instrument to sever the backbone or thicker bones of the fins. Cut the fish up into the size of steaks desired and wash lightly under the cold tap. If cutlets are required they can be sliced off in a similar fashion to cutting a loaf of bread. Hone the knife frequently, as knocking it or forcing it through the vertebrae and bones will quickly blunt the edge. Cutlet thickness will depend on individual taste and, more importantly, on the size of the fish. It is not really worth taking cutlets off a fish unless it is 3 lb or over. For this size, half-an-inch thick will do, but for larger fish, say 8 or 10 lb, thicker cutlets of an inch or so will prove ideal for cooking.

Preserving

Preserving fish these days generally means deep freezing, for the old arts of drying, salting and pickling have mostly died out. Before deep freezers were invented sea trout were dealt with in much more imaginative ways than today's convenient cold store in the garage. However, the freezer is such a handy way of keeping that sleek, silvery, fresh-run, five-pounder for a special occasion. How much nicer it is, also, to relive memories and on relating fishing tales to family or friends actually to be able to produce the evidence. I have known anglers who have kept a large fish for just that purpose, long past the time when it would have been fit to eat.

Whether to gut a whole fish before freezing depends largely on personal choice, even though to some it is a matter for controversial argument. Any fish which is likely to have some stomach contents should certainly be cleaned but sea trout caught in fresh water only very rarely contain food, so any danger of the flesh becoming tainted is remote. Some say that to leave a fish intact ensures a better flavour when eaten than one that has been gutted. I doubt whether that is the case, and gutted or not makes little or no difference in my opinion. Apart from the advantage already mentioned of being able to show the fish off in its whole and original state, the only fuel I can find to feed the argument is that it can be a simple task to gut a partially defrosted fish. When the outer flesh has defrosted the belly can be slit and the insides removed in a solid lump very easily with no mess whatsoever. This being a slight advantage on the side of the non-gutting lobby, I usually freeze my fish whole unless specifically asked to do otherwise.

A whole fish should be wrapped in a plastic bag, the air excluded and the bag sealed and labelled with the date and contents. A fish so dealt with within an hour or two of being caught will be preserved in first-class condition for at least six months and even up to twelve. Recommended freezer times for sea trout are lower than most fish, for it is oily like salmon, mackerel or herrings, and oil content is detrimental to long freezer life. Stale fish, that is fish which have been in the river some considerable time and begun to darken in colour, should not be kept for more than about six months even if frozen shortly after capture. The sealed plastic bag will prevent freezer burn which occurs quite readily in frozen fish.

With such valuable contents, the result of perhaps many hours of summer pleasure, deep-freeze insurance is essential. It is also as well to keep a periodic check on the temperature. A constant $-18°C$ or less should be maintained to preserve the contents in prime condition.

The fish can, of course, be conveniently frozen in portion-size fillets, steaks or cutlets ready for the table. Perhaps the slightly squeamish housewife will have forgotten the mess and gore after a time and will enjoy a cutlet or steak straight from the freezer to pan that much better. If the whole fish has been frozen it is not necessary to defrost all of it when a piece is required. With a clean, sharp tenon saw a steak of the required size can be simply sawn off. One word of warning, however, when sawing through a large fish, keep the saw moving, for a pause of only a few seconds will result in the saw freezing in position and then only a complete thaw out will remove it.

Smoking

In olden times preservation of fish was carried out in all parts of the world. Full advantage was taken of a seasonal glut, sometimes for only a short duration in the year for certain species, and as many fish were caught as possible. The bulk of the catch was then preserved by drying, salting or smoking, or in some instances a combination of all three, to provide food during the less productive times of the year. This dependence on fish was particularly true of the North American Indians whose camps and settlements grew up around the mouths of all the great salmon rivers and whose very existence depended upon the unfailing runs of these fish up the rivers to spawn.

Meat and fish can be preserved by drying. Depending as it did on the climate, this could not always be done, for fish and meat would have to be spread out and dried in the sun. Since micro-organisms which cause decomposition cannot grow in high concentrations of salt, salting was often used to preserve meat or fish. Drying or salting, however, meant that the meat required a considerable amount of preparation before it could be eaten.

A better method of preservation was, therefore, developed. This was smoking—a combination of drying and salting, which not only meant that the food was virtually ready to eat after being treated but also enhanced the flavour. Some smoked varieties of fish have become very popular and are frequently eaten, kippers and finnon haddock probably being the best known. Slowly becoming more popular are smoked mackerel, smoked eel and smoked trout (usually smoked rainbow trout from commercial fish farms).

Smoked sea trout and salmon have long been popular as appetisers. There is no reason why sea trout should not be just as good as salmon for this purpose. It has been said that smoked sea trout is inferior to salmon but also, conversely, that it is sweeter and has a more delicate flavour. The fact is that one would have to be something of an expert to tell the difference. Varieties of the Pacific salmon, such as Coho and Chinook and (dare I suggest) the odd large rainbow, now find their way on to the market as smoked salmon, and the taste varies little if they have been smoked properly.

There are various recipes for smoking fish, some closely guarded secrets using ingredients such as rum or other spirits, brown sugar (sugar also prevents growth of moulds and bacteria) or saltpetre as well as salt. The two basic methods are either cold smoking (the traditional way) or the more recent method of hot smoking.

When cold smoking, the fish is cured and not cooked. Large fish are filleted and small fish, like whitling, generally just gutted and smoked whole. The fish can either be left to steep in brine for about ten hours or covered in salt and left to dry for roughly the same period. It is then smoked without heat in special houses or chimneys for twelve hours or more. Various fuels are used, the best known being oak or beech sawdust, but some recipes use fresh-growing wood such as alder or holly. Haddock is traditionally cured over peat smoke.

Specialised knowledge is required to cold smoke sea trout successfully and the smokers are expensive to build or buy. For the angler who wishes to have his catch smoked it is better to take it to a smokery where for a reasonable fee (usually so much per pound weight) he can receive the fish back fully cured, the next day.

Hot smoking, where the fish is actually cooked and smoked at the same time over a much shorter period, is gaining in popularity. Small smokers can be purchased which normally consist of a metal box with a mesh griddle inside. The fish is prepared by gutting or filleting, wiped dry and spread liberally with salt and then placed on the griddle. A small amount of sawdust, which is supplied with the kit or can be bought separately at tackle shops, is sprinkled over the bottom of the box. A lid is put on the top and the container then placed over a methylated spirits burner which is set to burn for a predetermined length of time. After fifteen minutes or so, depending on the size of the smoker, the fish is ready for the table.

These small metal box smokers are quite easy to make. Half a biscuit tin over a primus stove is ideal and can be set up in the garden—fish smoking smells in the kitchen tend to linger. When camping such an easy and quick method of providing a delicious meal speaks for itself. These small hot smokers can also be used for meats like sausages or bacon.

Cooking

Many and varied are the ways of cooking sea trout. Any recipe for salmon can also be used, for they are very similar in taste and texture. Gourmets, however, claim that the sea trout has a more delicate flavour. One big advantage of sea trout is that they come in a greater variety of sizes, from small 8 oz fish, ideal for frying whole, to large, salmon-sized fish, fit to adorn a banqueting table. They can be boiled, steamed, baked, fried, grilled or made up into soups (chowders), pies, kedgerees or curries.

Boiled Boiled sea trout, sometimes called poached (it is really the same thing), is probably the easiest way of cooking large pieces. It can be eaten hot with new potatoes and parsley sauce, or left to cool and eaten cold with a salad of your choice. The piece to be cooked is best wrapped in a piece of muslin or, even better, in a parcel of grease-proof paper. Should it then be overcooked accidentally the whole will keep together and not fall to pieces. Bring to the boil a pan of enough salted water to cover the fish. Place the fish in it and then simmer, allowing ten minutes for each pound weight, plus ten minutes more. The salt is added to raise the boiling point temperature as much as to add to the flavour.

Be wary of ancient gourmet recipes which advise placing the fish in boiling water for a couple of minutes and then taking off the heat and leaving to cool; or even those that say on no account should the water ever boil. The worst damper to a dinner party or special occasion is to find that the main dish is not properly cooked.

To make a court bouillon (poaching liquor) for cooking whole sea trout the following recipe is traditional. To two pints of water add $\frac{1}{2}$ oz salt, four crushed peppercorns, two tablespoons vinegar, one bay leaf, one stalk of parsley and a sprig of thyme. Cover the pan and boil for thirty minutes. If poaching a whole, large fish in a court bouillon, place the fish in the liquor cold and bring gently up to the boil. Because of rapid shrinkage the skin of a whole fish would split and spoil its appearance if plunged straight into the boiling liquid. A fish of 5 lb needs to simmer for twenty minutes, and one of 8 lb for thirty minutes. When cooked the flesh, though still firm, will come away from the bone easily and cleanly. To test this, slide a knife down to the backbone at the lateral line and lever sideways.

One can experiment by poaching fish in wine or, as is the practice in France, by adding a varied selection of herbs to the cooking water, bay leaves and thyme being most frequently recommended to enhance the flavour.

As an alternative to boiling the fish may be steamed. A slightly longer cooking time is necessary—fifteen minutes for each pound weight, plus fifteen minutes extra, is about right. If a steamer is not available, the fish can be placed between two large dishes or soup plates and cooked over a pan of boiling water. A lemon sauce made of flour, milk, butter and lemon juice is recommended for steamed sea trout.

Baked Scale and gut a sea trout of 3 to 4 lb weight. Brush all the fish with melted butter, squeeze a little lemon juice over it, lightly season the inside and wrap the whole fish in buttered foil. Place in a large oven dish and bake for one hour at 350°F. Serve with the resulting sauce and the dish so produced is fit to set before a king. This is easily the best sea trout recipe and is so simple to cook and prepare. In Wales it is known as 'Sewin a saws menyn'. A sea trout (or salmon) cooked in such a way is ideal for placing on the table whole, hot or cold, and dressed with salad for a special occasion.

Fried Freshly caught whitling of 8 to 10 oz, fried with a little streaky bacon and served with new potatoes, are delicious. Before frying they can be coated with flour or bread crumbs but this is not really necessary if they are fried gently over a low heat. Seasoning with salt and pepper is important but not so much as to hide the flavour. The addition of a little lemon juice to such a dish is most tasty, as it is with many types of fried fish dishes.

Recipes

Trout with Bacon (Brithyll a Cig Moch)

4 whitling (8 to 10 oz each)
8 rashers streaky bacon
chopped parsley
butter
salt and pepper

Scale and gut the whitling, leaving the head, fins and tail intact. Season the insides. Brush each fish lightly with melted butter. Trim off the bacon rinds and lay the rashers flat in a baking dish. Lay the fish on top of the bacon at right angles. If cooking only a couple of fish, the rasher ends may be wrapped over the fish. Season lightly and garnish with chopped parsley. Cover the dish with cooking foil and bake in the oven for twenty minutes at 350°F (160°C).

Serve with new potatoes (tatws newydd) or, if not available, mash and parsley sauce (tatws stwns a saws persli). This dish is traditionally served with potato cakes (teisen datws) in north Wales.

Potato Cakes (Teisen Datws)

1 lb boiled mashed potatoes
4 oz flour with 1 teaspoon baking powder
1 egg
1 oz butter
1 tablespoon sugar
pinch of salt

Melt the butter and mix in all the ingredients. Roll out until about 1 inch thick (cut into shapes if desired) and bake for twenty minutes at 400°F (190°C).

Teifi Sea Trout with sauce (Teifi Sewin a saws)

1 lb of sewin fillets
4 oz butter
small glass of port
1 chopped anchovy
1 teaspoon tomato ketchup
salt and pepper

Clean the sea trout and fillet. Wash and dry the pieces and place in an oven dish. Season. Mix all the ingredients of the sauce, firstly melting the butter, and pour over the fillets. Cover the dish and bake for forty minutes at 375°F (170°C).

Sea Trout Fritters

4 oz cooked sea trout
4 slices of bread
1 teaspoon vinegar
2 oz self-raising flour
salt and pepper

Mash the sea trout in a bowl with the vinegar and seasoning. Spread over two slices of bread and place the other two slices on top as a sandwich. Cut into four. Prepare the batter, blending flour with water (add a pinch of salt). Coat the sandwiches with the batter and fry until golden brown on both sides. Serve wth tartar sauce and chipped potatoes or, alternatively, parsley sauce and mash.

Sea Trout Fish Cakes (Teisen Pyscod)

Many would consider it sacrilegious to use such a fine fish for making fish cakes. They are, however, a most palatable, easily prepared meal and are an ideal way of using up leftovers of cooked fish from a main meal. They can be very usefully frozen for later use.

10 oz mashed potato
6 oz cold, cooked sea trout
1 tablespoon chopped parsley

$\frac{1}{2}$ oz butter
salt and pepper

Mash the potatoes thoroughly and mix in the fish, finely-chopped parsley, melted butter and seasoning. Form into cakes on a floured board. To cook either coat with flour and shallow fry or brush with milk and place in a greased dish in the oven for fifteen minutes at 450°F (215°C).

Sea Trout Chowder

Use the leftover pieces of a large sea trout—fins, tail, bones and head (but not the offal).

1 large onion
1 oz butter
$\frac{1}{2}$ oz flour
8 oz potatoes
1 teaspoon vinegar
1 tablespoon chopped parsley
seasoning

Make half a pint of stock with the fish pieces: that is, boil until cooked, strain the liquid and then add any meat left on the bones to the stock. Chop the onion finely and fry in the butter until cooked. Add the whole to the stock, together with the potatoes, finely diced, and the vinegar. Blend in the flour and season to taste. Simmer for fifteen minutes and then add the chopped parsley. Cook for a further two minutes and serve piping hot. Add more stock if the mixture is too thick.

Sea Trout Pâté

8 oz cooked sea trout
1 oz butter
2 oz flour
$\frac{1}{2}$ oz finely chopped spring onion
$\frac{1}{2}$ oz finely chopped cooked carrots
1 teaspoon lemon juice
$\frac{1}{2}$ oz chopped parsley
salt, pepper and vinegar
cochineal (optional)
$\frac{1}{4}$ pint sea trout stock

Melt the butter in a saucepan, add the onion and the carrot. Fry gently for eight minutes. Add the stock and stir in the flour. Cook for three minutes. Mix in the flaked sea trout, lemon juice, parsley and a dash of vinegar and seasoning. Mix well while still hot. Add a little cochineal, if required, to give a darker pink colour. Place in an earthenware dish, preferably one with a lid, and allow to cool. When cold, garnish with sliced lemon and parsley.

Appendix

A ten-year analysis of sea trout catches by the author

I have always kept a record of all fish caught—not only salmon and sea trout, but sea fish like mullet, bass and even mackerel as well. Any success with the gun, be it pigeon, rabbit, duck or pheasant, also warrants an entry. Over a period of years this has enabled me to build up a valuable reference collection of where and when to expect prawns and crabs on the beach, the inshore migration of mullet and bass, the first shoals of mackerel, what the temperature has to rise to before it is worth setting the eel traps, and much, much more.

From these records I have gathered together the details on sea trout for the ten-year period from 1971 to 1980 inclusive. The information is listed in a series of histograms for easy reference and they are all set out as percentages of the totals relative to each particular table. This not only makes the tables more easily understood but helps to confine the data within the limits of the space available.

Table 10 shows that I caught a total of 1804 sea trout during the ten-year period. The high catch years of 1973 and 1975 do not necessarily mean that they were particularly good years for sea trout, and neither do the low figures for 1972 and 1979 imply that these were poor years. The catch effort was not constant from year to year. For instance in 1975, I lived close to a very good sea trout stretch on the river Teifi and fished regularly, while in 1977 I lived 200 miles away and fished only on rare occasions.

Over the period the fish caught came from the rivers Taf, Teifi, Aeron, Arth and Rheidol, but again the catch effort was not constant as there was no consistency of venue. In the first few years many fish came from the Taf and its tributaries, while towards the end they were almost exclusively Teifi and Aeron fish. The table in itself gives little or no useful information on catch statistics. However, the remaining graphs, which are based on it and break it down into different groups, show an enlightening insight into the varied but habitual lifestyle of sea trout in south-west Wales.

Table 11 gives monthly percentages of the total fish caught for the ten years. July is undoubtedly the best with over 35% of the total (647 fish) caught during that month. Only 1% were caught in May (21) and just over 10% (198) in June. August and September are the second and third best months, with the catch progressively tailing off. It is interesting to note that the figure of 4% (72 fish) for October represents only one week of fishing, the season closing each year on 7 October. For statistical purposes perhaps this figure should be multiplied by four (16%) to give a clearer picture of that month's catch. It may imply that October is a better month to fish than June but the fish are getting stale and losing condition at this time of year, compared with the sturdy fresh-run fish caught in May and June. Not only are the earlier fish fitter and stronger, providing top-class angling sport, but their eating qualities are far superior to the later models.

Tables 12 and 13 show the percentages of fish caught each month of under and over 2 lb. Though July is still, in each case, the best month, it can be seen that June is a good month for the larger fish, while August and September are better for the smaller. In May 3%, representing 9 fish, were caught over 2 lb, and 1% of the under 2 lb fish equals 12 individuals. This shows that on average in May for every three fish caught at least one will be over 2 lb. In June the ratio is similar, 74 to 124 fish respectively. In July, however, 35% of those over 2 lb (101 fish) are coupled with 36% of the under 2 lb category 546), which reveals that more than six fish need to be caught for every one in excess of 2 lb. The August figures reflect the large number of whitling running at this time and one can only expect a fish over 2 lb for every ten fish caught (44 to 425). By October figures of 14 and 60 reveal that the chances of a 2 lb + fish have risen again to one in five.

Table 14 gives the percentage of fish caught each year on a spinner, fly and worm respectively. Of the total of 1804 fish, 36% (649) were caught on a spinner, 54% (974) on a fly and 10% (181) on a worm. My favourite method is fly fishing at night and of the total caught on a fly, most of them were taken at this time. The years of 1971, 1973, 1974 and 1978 show 'normal' year profiles, with most fish being fly-caught, but with a fair average going to the spinner. It can be readily seen that the drier, low water summers, such as 1975, 1976 and 1980, produced a large percentage to the fly. Almost 75% of those caught in the drought year of 1976 were taken by this method. On the other hand, the wetter summers with plenty of floods and high water conditions, like 1972, 1977 and 1979, show a high proportion of fish caught on a spinner. The wet summer of 1972 produced an unusually large spinner total, though admittedly the number of fish caught that year is the lowest for the ten-year period.

Table 15 shows the monthly percentages of the total fish caught on a fly (974, or 54% of the total). July is by far the best month, with nearly 50%. June and August gave almost equal results. No fish were caught on a fly in October, which reflects the high water conditions that are unsuitable for fly fishing and which are usually experienced at this time of the year.

Of the fish caught on a spinner shown in table 16 (649 or 36% of the total) July, August and September show almost equal results. Again, if the October figures were multiplied by four, this month's results would also compare favourably—around 20%.

Table 17 represents 181 fish (10% of the total) caught on a worm. These were almost all caught in heavy, coloured water, as I do not fish with a worm at night when undoubtedly most fish are caught by this method. Little pattern emerges, apart from the fact that over 70% were caught in August and September. This may be because more floods are experienced during these months than during June or July, or that being at the height of the sea trout run there are more fish in the river at that time. No fish were caught on a worm in October. It does not mean that October is a poor month. With the salmon runs in Wales becoming ever later I am concentrating more on that species at this time; in some years it seems to be the only chance of getting a couple for the freezer.

To summarise, the figures suggest that for fly fishing the earlier part of the season is best. Most fish were caught in July, with June being the second best month. August and September show a gradual reduction in sport and for the whole of the ten-year period no fish were caught on a fly in October. The heavy water almost invariably experienced during that month produces poor fly fishing conditions. For spinning, fish were caught in each month from May to October, but the best months giving equal results are July, August and September, with a consistent 30% of the total in each. The 5% caught in October reflects the good spinning water normally encountered in that month.

Fish were caught on a worm in each month except October, with August and September being equal best.

Table 10: Number of sea trout caught per season for ten years from 1971 to 1980.

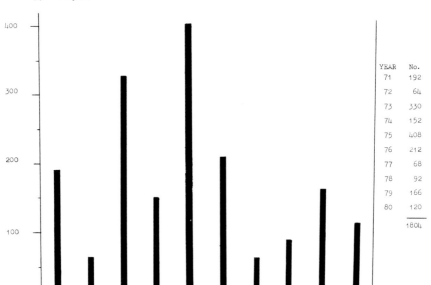

YEAR	No.
71	192
72	64
73	330
74	152
75	408
76	212
77	68
78	92
79	166
80	120
	1804

Table 11: Monthly percentages of total number of fish caught.

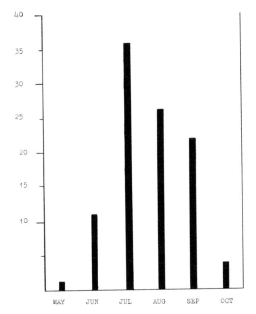

MAY	1%	21
JUN	11%	198
JUL	36%	647
AUG	26%	469
SEP	22%	397
OCT	4%	72
		1804

Table 12: Monthly percentages of fish caught under 2 lb (1516).

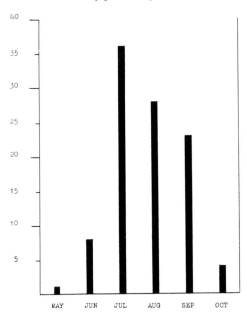

MAY	1%	12
JUN	8%	124
JUL	36%	546
AUG	28%	425
SEP	23%	349
OCT	4%	60
		1516

Table 13: Monthly percentages of fish caught over 2 lb (288).

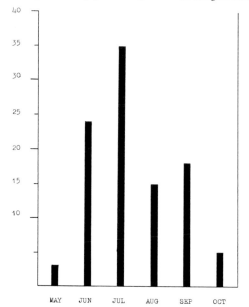

Monthly percentag
over 2 lb (288)

MAY	3%	9
JUN	24%	74
JUL	35%	101
AUG	15%	44
SEP	18%	48
OCT	5%	12
		———
		288

Table 14: Annual percentages of sea trout caught on spinner, fly and worm.

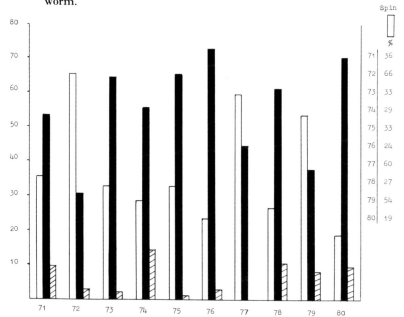

	Spin	Fly	Worm
	%	%	%
71	36	54	10
72	66	31	3
73	33	65	2
74	29	56	15
75	33	66	1
76	24	73	3
77	60	40	0
78	27	62	11
79	54	38	8
80	19	71	10

Table 15: Monthly percentages of fish caught on a fly (974).

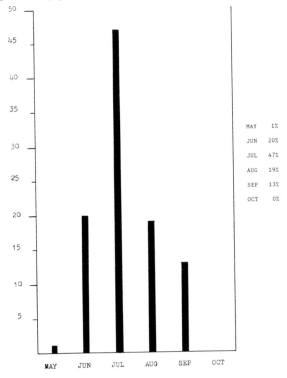

MAY	1%
JUN	20%
JUL	47%
AUG	19%
SEP	13%
OCT	0%

Table 16: Monthly percentages of fish caught on a spinner (649).

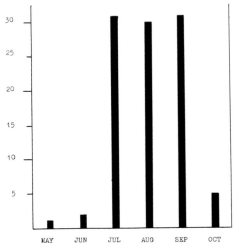

MAY	1%
JUN	2%
JUL	31%
AUG	30%
SEP	31%
OCT	5%

Table 17: Monthly percentages of fish caught on a worm (181).

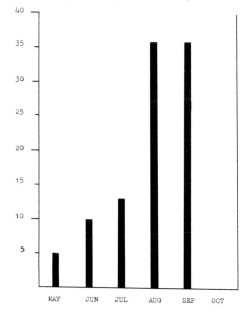

MAY	5%
JUN	10%
JUL	13%
AUG	36%
SEP	36%
OCT	0%

Glossary

Adipose fin	A small, fleshy fin between the dorsal fin and the tail
Alevin	A newly hatched fish with the yolk sac attached
Ammocoete	The young larval form of lampreys
Anadromous	Fish which migrate from salt water to fresh water to spawn
Anal fin	The fin underneath the body behind the vent
Blastoderm	The cluster of cells in an egg which will form the embryo
Borland	A type of lock fish-pass over large obstructions
Brith y dail	(Welsh) Meaning 'speckled like the leaves': an autumn run sea trout
Brithyl	(Welsh) Trout
Brych y dail	(Welsh) An autumn run sea trout
Bull trout	A darkly-coloured, late-running sea trout
Carnivorous	Flesh-eating
Cast	The section of line nearest the bait; the leader
Caudal	Of the tail
Caudal fin	The tail fin
Caudal peduncle	The tapering section of the body just forward of the tail
Circuli	The concentric ring growth marks on a scale
Clutch	The adjustable tension on the spool of a spinning reel
Cutting	Making a redd by excavating a nest in gravel
Denil	A type of baffled fish-pass with a water flow of constant velocity
Dorsal	Of the back, the top side
Dorsal fin	The large rayed fin on the back
Embryo	The early stage of development inside the egg
Eutrophic	A productive water rich in animal and plant life
Fertilisation	The moment of union between sperm and egg
Finnock	A sea trout (north Scotland)
Flood	Heavy, muddy and excessive river flow after rainfall
Foul-hooked	A fish hooked other than in the mouth
Fry	A young fish
Gab	The smooth water at the tail of a pool
Gill arch	The cartilage support of the gill filaments
Gill cover	The operculum: the flap-like cover of the gills

Gill filament	The slender fringes of the gill
Gill rakers	Bony protrusions on the gill arches
Gills	The organs of respiration
Glide	A smooth run of even depth
Gonads	The organs of reproduction: female—ovaries; male —testes
Herling	A sea trout (Solway district, also Cumbria)
Lateral line	A line of sensory pores along the side of a fish
Leader	A cast
Lie	A position in a pool where fish rest or remain stationary
Maxilla	The long bone at the side of the upper jaw
Mending	Looping a floating fly line upstream to counteract current drag on the fly
Micropyle	Hole on the egg surface to admit a spermatozoon
Milt	Sperm
Necrosis	Death of tissue
Oligotrophic	(opp: *eutrophic*) An unproductive, usually acid, barren water
Operculum	The gill cover
Osmosis	The movement of water from a weak solution to a strong solution across a semi-permeable membrane
Otter	A device for releasing caught-up baits
Ova	(sing: *ovum*) Fish eggs
Ovaries	The female reproductive organs.
Parr	A sea trout during its juvenile river life
Parr marks	Distinctive row of finger marks on a parr's flanks
Peal	A sea trout (Devon) or a sea trout smolt (west Wales)
Pectoral fins	The paired fins nearest the head
Pelvic fins	The paired fins nearest the tail
pH	A measure of the alkalinity or acidity of a water
Photosynthesis	A process whereby oxygen is given off by submerged plants during the daytime
Pit	A redd (Ireland)
Pool	Part of a river, deeper than average, where a fish will lie
Redd	A salmonid's nest: an excavation in the gravel where eggs are laid
Respiration	A process whereby oxygen is taken up and carbon dioxide is given off by submerged plants during darkness
Riffle	A shallow, fast run with dimpled surface
Rise	A fish coming up to the surface to take a fly or volume of river water increasing after rainfall
Roe	The eggs of fish
Rough	A stretch of fast, broken water
Run	The act of a fish seizing a lure; a number of sea trout entering a river at the same time; a stretch or river of even width and depth intermediary between riffle and pool

Schoolie	A whitling
Sewin	A sea trout (Welsh)
Shoal sewin	Whitling
Sewin bach	A small sea trout; a whitling (Welsh)
Side strain	When playing a fish, applying pressure from the side to turn it away from its direction of travel
Smolt	A parr that has turned silver and is ready to migrate to the sea
Snag	An obstruction on the river bed where a bait is liable to get caught up
Spate	A flood
Sperm	Seminal fluid containing the spermatozoa; milt
Spermatozoon	The male cell of reproduction
Spinner	Any lure that is drawn through the water at depth not being a 'fly'
Stickle	A small area of fast, turbid water
Stockie bashing	The art (?) of catching newly-stocked trout in a reservoir or lake
Strike	A sharp pull on the line to secure the hook hold or a run
Stripping	Artificially taking spawn from a fish; drawing a fly in rapidly by hand
Swim bladder	A gas-filled sac in the body cavity
Tail	The shallow water at the downstream end of a pool; the caudal fin
Tail, to	To grasp a fish by the caudal wrist
Take	A run
Tension	The amount of pull required to release the clutch on a fixed spool reel
Testes	The male reproductive organs
Tumble	To cause a fish to move at a spinner but not touch it
Tumbling	A hooked sea trout flapping on the surface of fast water
Turn	To tumble a fish
Twps y dail	(Welsh) Meaning 'stupid with the leaves': an autumn sea trout
Vent	The external opening of the alimentary canal
White trout	A sea trout (Ireland)
Whitling	A sea trout returning to the river in the same year as smolt migration
Yolk	The food part of an egg
Yalk sac	The appendage attached to the stomach of an alevin from whence it gets its food

Index